#NousSommes

Modern French Identities

Edited by Jean Khalfa

Volume 135

PETER LANG
Oxford · Bern · Berlin · Bruxelles · New York · Wien

Susie Cronin, Sofia Ropek Hewson
and Cillian Ó Fathaigh (eds)

#NousSommes

Collectivity and the Digital in
French Thought and Culture

PETER LANG
Oxford · Bern · Berlin · Bruxelles · New York · Wien

Bibliographic information published by Die Deutsche Nationalbibliothek
Die Deutsche Nationalbibliothek lists this publication in the Deutsche Nationalbibliografie; detailed bibliographic data is available on the Internet at http://dnb.d-nb.de.

A catalogue record for this book is available from the British Library.

Library of Congress Cataloging-in-Publication data:

Names: Cronin, Susie, 1991– editor. | Ropek Hewson, Sofia, 1991- editor. | Ó Fathaigh, Cillian, 1992- editor.
Title: #noussommes : collectivity and the digital in French thought and culture / Susie Cronin, Sofia Ropek Hewson, Cillian Ó Fathaigh.
Description: First edition. | Oxford ; New York : Peter Lang, 2020. | Includes bibliographical references and index. |
Identifiers: LCCN 2019021093 | ISBN 9781788747677
Subjects: LCSH: Internet—Social aspects—France. | France—Intellectual life.
Classification: LCC HN440.I56 N68 2019 | DDC 302.23/10944—dc23
LC record available at https://lccn.loc.gov/2019021093

Cover image: Classic Paris Terrace. Photo by Charles Loyer on Unsplash.
Cover design by Peter Lang Ltd.

ISSN 1422-9005
ISBN 978-1-78874-767-7 (print) • ISBN 978-1-78874-768-4 (ePDF)
ISBN 978-1-78874-769-1 (ePub) • ISBN 978-1-78874-770-7 (mobi)

© Peter Lang AG 2020

Published by Peter Lang Ltd, International Academic Publishers,
52 St Giles, Oxford, OX1 3LU, United Kingdom
oxford@peterlang.com, www.peterlang.com

Susie Cronin, Sofia Ropek Hewson and Cillian Ó Fathaigh have asserted their right under the Copyright, Designs and Patents Act, 1988, to be identified as Editors of this Work.

All rights reserved.
All parts of this publication are protected by copyright.
Any utilisation outside the strict limits of the copyright law, without the permission of the publisher, is forbidden and liable to prosecution. This applies in particular to reproductions, translations, microfilming, and storage and processing in electronic retrieval systems.

This publication has been peer reviewed.

Contents

Acknowledgements   vii

SUSIE CRONIN, SOFIA ROPEK HEWSON AND CILLIAN Ó FATHAIGH
Introducing #NousSommes   1

PATRICIA MACCORMACK
'Who is this we that is not me?': Ecosophical Ethics   9

SOLANGE MANCHE
#WeAreTheEarth: Rethinking Ecology and Community:
The Case of Humanist Anarchism   27

BOUBÉ YACOUBA SALIFOU
Je suis Charlie: entre émotion et identité sociopolitique   41

ALEXANDRE LESKANICH
'The metamorphosis of the world into man': The Anthropocene
and the Historical Administration of Human Identity   55

JACK COOPEY
Walter Benjamin's Arcades Project as the #NousSommes of
Social Media   75

MARIE CHABBERT
Liberté, égalité ... Totalité? Décrypter les dangers de *#JeSuis*
avec Jean-Luc Nancy   85

BENOÎT LE BOUTEILLER

Un *nous* contemporain: réseaux sociaux, discours nouveau et addiction 101

MARIANNE GODARD

La communauté comme passage: l'éthique du poème d'Henri Meschonnic 117

ANDREA PERUNOVIC

#NousSommes: refondation onto-axiologique de la confiance 129

#NousSommes and Automatic Politics: An Interview with Martin Crowley 141

Notes on Contributors/Notes sur les auteurs 157

Index 161

Acknowledgements

This publication emerged from the twentieth annual French Graduate Conference, held at Pembroke College, Cambridge, in May 2017. The conference received generous financial support from the Society for French Studies, Pembroke College, and both the Department of French and the School of Arts and Humanities at the University of Cambridge, for which we are very grateful. This conference would not have been possible without the endless help and assistance of Bill Burgwinkle. We would like to thank Laurel Plapp and Simon Phillimore at Peter Lang for all their kind support and patience. We are grateful to Edinburgh University Press for permission to reproduce Patricia MacCormack's article. Finally, we would like to thank Ian James, Peter Collier and Martin Crowley, whose support was invaluable in developing the publication.

SUSIE CRONIN, SOFIA ROPEK HEWSON AND CILLIAN Ó FATHAIGH

Introducing #NousSommes

#JeSuisCharlie. #WeAreOrlando. #NousSommesStrasbourg. These are simply a few examples of a new idiom and phenomenon that has emerged, whereby the 'personal' modalities of social media become embroiled in collective expressions of unity, solidarity and resistance. How do we read these digital signifiers? These hashtags bear attachments of grief, pity, trauma, pain, but also represent messages of collectivity, community, courage, strength and hope. The meaning of these apparently simple formulations is fundamentally ambiguous. While these hashtags may at one and the same time appear clear and univocal, and have reached the point of almost constituting one of multiple forms of expected responses to traumatic events, they also open up new and fundamental questions about violence, trauma, collectivity and identity in the age of the digital. What makes these articulations particular, and what makes the digital dimension worthy of special attention in its scope for accommodating articulations of solidarity, struggle, despair on the one hand, and hope, collectivity, community on the other? Does the digital hold this power on account of its limitlessness, its intangibility, its ability to inspire utopian rewritings as a kind of space beyond the present, the immediate, physical world? This volume seeks to address these issues from a rich diversity of angles, precisely converging around the theme of #NousSommes/#WeAre.

It was only four years ago, on 7 January 2015, that the *Charlie Hebdo* terrorist attack took place. Twelve people were killed, and eleven were injured. The tragedy was met by political, social and communal responses, and from this density of commentary and response emerged the hashtag #JeSuisCharlie. This first-person singular attached itself to the symbol of *Charlie*. In this we saw the cohesion of a multiplicity around one single symbol. The dissemination of this hashtag had important, explicit political effects whose various manifestations included that of forty-four world leaders joining arms in a rally following the attack. And, yet, like these world leaders, the unification around this symbol was a confused one, vulnerable to differing interpretations. Diffracting and multiplying into various articulations, the tag began to appear in the unification of other groupings, which saw the emergence of tags such as #JeSuisJuif or #JeSuisUnPolicier. More than this prolific multiplication of reiterations, this apparently unified wave of solidarity, however, the sharing and adoption of these terms concealed broad alignment with a rather noble, albeit nebulous, set of values. The sharing and usage of #JeSuis and similar tags gestured at once to a defence of free speech, support for a presumed parcel of 'Western' values, a protest against terrorism and violence, and a desire for safety. While this movement of #JeSuisCharlie brought people together, outstretching limbs to and from various corners of cyberspace, it also masked the divisions behind this apparent (re)iteration of agreement and solidarity.

Indeed, this proliferation of alliances was not limited to the singular, but broadened into the first-person plural: #WeAreOrlando following a fatal shooting in the United States, as well as #NousSommesStrasbourg. Here, the issue of collectivity was articulated more explicitly. Rather than simply being a unification around the symbol of *Charlie*, this appealed to a plural identity, an identity both pre-established before the event, but also partially determined by its resistance to such an event. Unlike the symbolic movement in *Charlie*, this 'we' had fewer connections to abstract values (such as free speech) and instead referenced the city as its identity. It would be a mistake to draw a hard distinction between the singular and the plural here. However, it remains the case that this movement away from the singular brought these questions of collectivity into sharp relief. If we privilege the 'nous' within our title, it is precisely in order to emphasise the digital aspects of this communal question.

Despite their many advantages in formulating new communities and modes of expression, social media offer neither an independent public space nor one that is immune to the questions of power and hierarchy. Indeed, entranced by the false sense of security and freedom experienced by many individuals in their use of social media as a personal tool of expression, user engagement typically neglects to consider the ways in which online spaces and modalities of 'sharing' are far from unbiased. Social media are then best not naively assumed to function simply as sites for identities to form freely and spontaneously, but are on the other hand sites in which identities may relatively easily be manipulated, reassigned and corrupted. Cyberdemocracy has proven itself not to be free from the problems of democracy in the more tangible world; if anything, new and more elaborate issues have arisen in the transposition of freedoms and contributions into this new and unfamiliar space. The outstanding requirements and issues of managing equality of expression in online space have been brought into focus by recent political campaigns, whereby rather than enriching knowledge, the internet has also been seen to have opened up a space for misinformation, fake news and anonymous, malicious influences. As is the case with regards to any expression in any medium, the question of *whom* is speaking, from *where* and *why* was never far behind.

One of the common critiques employed against 'online activism' is that the manifestation of affect seen in a hashtag does not materialise into corresponding, real political manifestations in 'public'. Noise is made, in other words, around buzzwords and issues, but little or nothing is changed in the 'real world' by this digital outcry. Certainly, the act of sharing a hashtag does not necessarily amount to a substantial political commitment. That said, in the case of certain phenomena, such as the #MeToo movement, there are still very real political effects and developments that follow from these online, 'shared' forms of social media activism. Online spaces provide areas through which considerable 'traffic' passes, making a pronouncement on a prominent platform akin to a public occupation in a main city square, with the lifting of any geographical restrictions. As such, the power of social media as platforms for spreading certain political and social messages is indubitable. While the hashtag #NousSommes may not be an identical form of public manifestation as a protest, then, we aim to explore the possibilities and pitfalls of digital gatherings. Our aim in this volume is to consider the public and political importance of such forms of protest, as well as to elaborate new ways of understanding the offering of online tools and platforms to processes of identity formation and assertion.

While articulations like #NousSommes carry within them an important, and often unrecognised, degree of political agency and potential, it is also difficult to escape the traumatic passivity on which they are based. These words are issued and spurted as responses to trauma, repeated oftentimes more in persistent incredulity than in empowered resistance and conviction. What marks the singularity of #NousSommes and kindred movements is the role of the digital in mediating this trauma. Both our experience of traumatic events, such as terrorist attacks, and our response to them become embedded in a new virtual element. Our experience of these events is not simply broadcast through television and other media, media of which we are the recipients, but our response to them has also become partially determined by the digital, media that endow us with dual entitlements and responsibilities as consumers and contributors. While seeking to take into account the important and recent change that has occurred in the incorporation of the digital as a voice through which trauma, identity and solidarity may be articulated, it is also vital to avoid collapsing into an opposition, which considers these digital processes as somehow derivative or artificial. We are convinced that these hashtags need to be understood as part of a collective process of negotiating traumatic events, but one which challenges both our understanding of the collective and our understanding of the trauma.

It is important for us to stress the novelty and urgency of the discourses with which this volume seeks to engage. While such modes of expression may have first prominently manifested themselves in #JeSuisCharlie, this has not prevented them from developing thereafter. In many ways, digital articulations of community, grief and belonging are still very much an emerging phenomenon and one that has changed substantially even since the #NousSommes/#WeAre conference took place in Cambridge in May 2017. It is precisely because of this that we need to think through these. With increasing frequency and importance, these digital manifestations are becoming part of our public space. This volume seeks to capture this urgency and both engage with the already determined versions of this #NousSommes, as well as the potentials and possibilities contained within it. Importantly, these potentials are not limited to the specific phenomenon of these hashtags, but also greater questions around the digital, the collective, trauma, the human, and the machine.

Novelty and urgency also characterise another narrative which shapes this volume: the 'Anthropocene'. The Anthropocene is a proposed new epoch that encompasses the impact of human activity on the Earth. The Anthropocene Working Group presented their recommendation to the International Geological Congress in 2016 on the basis that nuclear testing, pollution, deforestation and development, among many other factors, have altered Earth beyond the stability denoted by the Holocene – our current geological age. This volume approaches the Anthropocene cautiously and critically, analysing the problems associated with placing human activity at the centre of our geological and cultural narratives. These problems might include our persistent othering of animals, expressed by a number of contributors in this volume, or an identity crisis produced by our inability to comprehend or take control of this new epoch – despite its emphasis on our intervention and impact. Ultimately, the Anthropocene forces us to rethink community and agency: understanding the #NousSommes produced by the Anthropocene is a crucial part of understanding this new epoch.

One further compelling facet is the unique cultural interaction that this #NousSommes has provoked. Our contributors come from multiple different countries and are informed by a rich diversity of contexts, and the volume itself seeks to articulate a mixture of Francophone and Anglophone approaches. That said, there is a strong focus on the resources of French culture in addressing this question. This is not simply because of the French origin of the #JeSuisCharlie; rather, it is also a product of a particular focus on the thinking of the social and political within (particularly twentieth-century) French philosophy, literature and film.

Above all else, what we have sought to bring together in this volume is a multi-disciplinary perspective, which both demonstrates the rich depths and ever-expanding frontiers of the field of French Studies, while also demonstrating all that the field has to gain from dialogue with 'external' disciplines and non-traditional themes. Our work as editors has been based on a strong belief that this emerging concept of digital collectivity requires the perspectives to be gained from drawing upon multiple disciplines. While this may be so, it is not possible to address the essence of #NousSommes without rethinking the origins of the boundaries within which these disciplines have been established, and indeed on whose preservation they have traditionally depended for their survival. What is the relationship of the community to the outside, and how is its relevance changing in this age of the digital, itself hardly any longer a 'new' age? It is our hope that

Contributions

To begin, Patricia MacCormack explores nonhuman and queer theories of subjectivity. MacCormack analyses animals, art and the Anthropocene in the context of these theories in order to progress new ways of understanding our relationship with our environment, and new ways of living which promote relationality rather than colonisation or occupation. Discussions of anthropocentrism and the fetishisation of the non-human are central to her development of a new ethics.

Solange Manche analyses anarchist humanism in the context of Murray Bookchin's theories of social ecology. Manche posits that the exploitation characteristic of the Anthropocene can be explained through 'the torture scheme': a competitive neoliberal work ethic in which inflicting and suffering pain are elided. Manche approaches the Anthropocene through the frame of human exploitation, as a facet of geological exploitation.

Though #JeSuisCharlie may have begun in the West, it is important to stress that this phenomenon and its effects are not limited to the West. Boubé Yacouba Salifou's work carefully outlines the effects of #JeSuisCharlie and the relation between us and them that this can instigate within a postcolonial context. This chapter takes as its object the reception of #JeSuisCharlie in the Republic of the Niger and considers both the intermingling of identities and affective attachments that this generated. Yacouba Salifou's chapter helps us better understand the important question of the reception of these hashtags, but also the complex relationship between the Republic of the Niger and France.

Alexandre Leskanich examines the Anthropocene in the context of administration, comprehension and identity. Leskanich describes this new epoch as 'incarcerating' in its subsuming of all planetary activity under human control and management. Leskanich explores how this human-centred narrative makes it harder for us to understand ourselves and our environment, and leaves us unable to address the ecological challenges inherent to the Anthropocene.

An essential way to address a new phenomenon is to seek models in the past. Jack Coopey's chapter seeks to sketch out the links between Walter Benjamin and #NousSommes. Coopey offers an account of Benjamin's *Arcades Project* and links this to our present relationship to social media. The chapter foregrounds the way in which collective agency and consciousness can be developed through idioms like #NousSommes. Building on the Marxist conception of alienation, Coopey suggests that this new technology needs to be understood dialectically in order to bring outs its emancipatory potential.

Marie Chabbert's article draws upon the work of Jean-Luc Nancy in an approach that unpicks some of the potential issues surrounding the formation of communities through digital unifiers. Chabbert indicates the issues generated by ostensible articulations of inclusivity, reminding us all too necessarily that inclusion almost always presupposes its opposite. Examining the particular case of the French context, and the movement surrounding the *Charlie Hebdo* attacks and subsequent proliferation of #NousSommes, Chabbert signals the dangerous homogeneity of said movement.

Many of these articles touch on or allude to the affective dimension of attachment and collectivity; however, this also raises questions about a psychoanalytic approach. Benoît le Bouteiller addresses just this question. Drawing on his clinical work, le Bouteiller considers the relationship between social media, addiction and the formation of collective identities. Building on the work of Jacques Lacan, le Bouteiller draws out the psychoanalytical implications for these new media and our dependence on them. Moreover, this chapter considers the implications of this dependence for concrete political events, namely the election of Bolsonaro in Brazil in 2018. In so doing, le Bouteiller's work brings out the clear political and psychological problematics in the formation of new collectives.

Marianne Godard approaches the notion of community through a literary, and specifically poetic, perspective. The 'Nous' of Henri Meschonnic's 'Nous le passage' echoes and preempts movements such as #NousSommes, insofar as the work attempts to verbally and poetically weave a space of communality, an anonymous singular subject is offered by Meschonnic as a way of thinking the 'nous.'

This thinking of collectivity also raises fundamental philosophical questions. Andrea Perunovic brings these forward around the question of confidence. Engaging with key thinkers in French thought, particularly Nancy and Derrida, this chapter teases out the potential for a rethinking of our 'being-with-others' through #NousSommes. For Perunovic, social media offers the potential to rethink the foundations of our sociality and the confidence that we have in one another.

Finally, this collection concludes with an interview with Martin Crowley. Crowley's interview expands on his work on the concept of automatic politics. Here, not only do we see the important political stakes of #NousSommes, but also our potential for activism and resistance through the internet and social media. Crowley builds lucidly on a number of different French philosophers (most notably Bernard Stiegler) to consider what happens to our politics in an age of automation and what this entails for equality, emancipation and community.

These chapters all approach #NousSommes from a diverse set of viewpoints and theoretical positions. It is our hope that this collection will help foster debate around the role that the humanities, and particularly French Studies, have in relation to digital media. Only through careful, rigorous and collective thinking can we hope to fully understand the implications and possibilities of #NousSommes.

PATRICIA MACCORMACK

'Who is this we that is not me?': Ecosophical Ethics[1]

> It is not sufficient to liberate sexuality; it is also necessary to liberate ourselves from the notion of sexuality itself.
> — Foucault (2000: 245)

> This *man of negation* – yes, even he counts among the very great forces which *conserve* and *affirm* life ... What is the reason for this sickliness? For man is more sick, more uncertain, more mutable, less defined than any other animal ... even when this master of destruction, of self-destruction *wounds* himself – it is the wound itself which afterwards compels him to *live* ...
> — Nietzsche (1996: 100)

> Already constructed theoretical language does not speak of the mucous. The mucous remains a remainder, producer of delirium, of dereliction, of wounds, sometimes of exhaustion.
> — Irigaray (2002a: 244)

> That is the only way Nature operates – against itself.
> — Deleuze and Guattari (1987: 242)

The above quotations share a disparagement of three systems: the system of epistemic language, the system of a non-relational hermeneutic man separate from the world, and the system which paradoxically claims that one's capacity to define and be a subject leads to one's freedom through that subjectivity. The nonhuman haunts all of these criticisms. It is present not as a precursor to the human in a chrono-centric pre-evolutionary way, nor as a descriptor of any organism which fails to fulfil the criteria of the human (itself a myth which has been anxiously affirmed and debunked

---

1   This article first appeared as 'Art, Nature, Ethics: Nonhuman Queerings', *Somatechnics*, Vol. 5: Issue 2, 2015. Thanks to Edinburgh University Press for their permission to reproduce it.

since its inception). It is present as the world, even the cosmos, itself. Its verb-like (or active) affect precedes its function as a noun. It may describe any organism in a state which expresses and is affected in ways resistant to the three systems mentioned above, but it more describes escape routes, or modes of being which are apprehended in their more 'natural' state, though nature is not pitted against culture but is, rather, everything in its chaotic state, the pure potentiality of all mechanisms and combinations for action, production, destruction and metamorphosis. As Deleuze and Guattari tell us, nature operates against itself because it is not an 'it' in the same way that man or human is phantasised desperately as such. Nature is infinite particles and waves that include all matter without demarcating anything as independent of its connections to all other matter. The wounded man of Nietzsche is not destroyed but opened out towards novel possibilities of penetration and reformation, via the becoming-mucosal of Irigaray's delirium and dereliction, mucus being a thoroughly nonhuman and thoroughly natural substance, a posthuman or ahuman humour, perhaps.

What trajectories of expression could constitute a nonhuman? I posit three: The nonhuman is constituted as an ethical entity without co-option or fetishisation; the nonhuman is a work of art as a silent, unknowable falsehood; the nonhuman is a work of nature in that it is the thought of nature. The first can only be a result of the experimentations of the second and third and thus will be addressed last.

Nonhuman as Art

In *The Genealogy of Morals*, Nietzsche sees art as having two principles: the first is it cannot operate to fulfil criteria and thus resolve or heal a problem. Related to this, the second principle is that art as falsehood shows the world as error. These both come from Man's tragic adherence to the concept of the ideal where he asks 'Is an ideal being set up or broken down here?' (1996: 75). The first principle shows the folly in attempts to glue together the broken ideal, the second that ideals are erroneous understandings of the world to begin with. Beyond their associations with diachronous qualities of good and bad, ideals order the world through a will to power that privileges power over affect. This will to power also subsumes freedom, as an affirmation of a perceived understanding of the one who imposes that force as superior subject. The idealisation of the 'I' slaughters freedom before action even begins, and attempts at recuperation slaughter creativity. The vitalism in Nietzsche's understanding of art, even though Deleuze calls it tragic (2006: 95), shows that Man's tragedy comes paradoxically from his attempt to understand himself through force as power, and his expression of force without creativity as ultimately destroying other possible creative relations, and showing his ideal as a myth. The falsity of art, the world as an error, is a jubilantly positive way to describe art's function. We understand the world through humanism as a topography populated with demarcated truths waiting to be illuminated, and which will all gel into a logical jigsaw and thus illuminate our own existences upon this topos when we finally reveal these truths. This self-perpetuating force relies on the pseudo-religious sense in science of logic as being coincident with meaning. Understanding the world as error repudiates the myth of logocentrism and relishes the inexhaustibility of the world in its perpetual recombinings of relations and the affects they produce. Via Irigaray with Nietzsche, error sometimes produces wounds, and these are the openings, or corporeally and psychically (never extricated of course) beneficial escape routes via which our new and unexpected becomings occur. Error is defined via man, and as Deleuze and Guattari state, nature operates against itself: for nature this is harmony, for man this is discord. Disjunctive combinations of things brought together 'in error' or 'unnaturally' as humanism may describe them, are the artistic combinations available only via nonhuman trajectories – those which are done with ideals, done with human faith in logocentrism, done with any form of art as recuperative or a more perfected form of nature, as Artaud says, to be done with the judgement of (State, Family, Capital, Education as) God: 'The fact that the world is not yet formed,/Or that man only has a small idea of the world/and wants to hold onto it forever?/This comes from the fact that man,/one fine day,/stopped/the idea of the world' (1988: 561).

Without wishing to draw false polarities, what Nietzsche and Artaud emphasise is that the human comes to the world from a psychical, ideational structuring of the world and by this actualisation of the world never experiences world, or self, or most explicitly self as infinite and infinitesimal part of the world. The nonhuman coming to the world as part of the world and already within the world is simultaneously corporeal and psychical (we are also done with the judgement of Descartes) and, most explicitly, undifferentiated from the world, including all other organisms and the unknowable of self within self – the word 'self' becoming an increasingly tenuous term. While this notion of undifferentiated relation resonates with queer theory, it also brings queer theory and art together. Nietzsche tells us what art is not for, and celebrates falsehood, yet from a nonhuman perspective, falsehood is nothing more than forsaking the idea of truth and falsity and their isomorphic hierarchical dissymmetry. Deleuze states that for the dogmatic definition of thought and image in art: 'We are also told that we are diverted from the truth but by forces which are foreign to it (body, passions, sensuous interests)' (2006: 96). By this dogma truth has its acolyte adherents – the very humans who created the concept to begin with, as a will to power, not an observation of 'reality' (itself often highly unreal). Any forces which are antagonistic to humanist thought must therefore be antagonistic to truth. Art, by its constructed nature, is untrue. While dogma sees this as resolvable through 'method' (Deleuze, 2006: 96) which makes logical our relations with nature, any 'method' opposed to logic would be untrue, and yet it is these methods which create and are responsible for art that liberates thought as an opening rather than confers information or knowledge as a structuring.

Queering the nonhuman could be considered an artistic practice for two reasons: the first is the impossible bind that we are in human culture and our access to nature is fatally prevented by this state, yet we must try liberate ourselves from this mode of apprehension for the sake of art and other nonhuman organisms, specifically the other lives we destroy. Secondly, acknowledging falsehood makes all things true, creating the queer relation as a chaos magic mantra in the hope that the expressions we emit and the affects we produce will fulfil the function of art – not to represent or confirm but to open new modes of expressivity in those which encounter art.

For, like nature, art operates against itself. Deleuze explicitly states that dogma critiques the body, passions and sensuous interests. However these intensities manifest the body as ecstatic and vulnerable. Shifting from 'the' body, externally evaluated and judged by God, to body as constellation of intensities, independent of inside/outside, object/subject, describes the body as expressive and affective, liberated from the myth of the human, Vitruvian template which coincides with identity itself. Artaud explores this simultaneous destruction as liberation of body and subject as:

> The need to abolish the idea,/the idea and its myth,/ and to enthrone in its place/ the thundering manifestation/ of this explosive necessity:/to dilate the body of my internal night,/ the internal nothingness/ of myself/ which is night,/ nothingness, /thoughtlessness,/but which is explosive affirmation/that there is/ something/to make room for: my body. (Artaud 1988: 565)

The body as Body without Organs, more correctly without organisation, for Artaud is the site of life, nature and freedom but his use of words shows, like many writers such as Bataille, Cixous, Irigaray and Kristeva, words can manifest corporeality without becoming ideals, words are fleshy mucosal bodies, Irigaray's language of delirium. Art shows all substances as corporeal and also connects the cosmos with its own unique substance that is irrefutably libidinal, but without an object of desire: 'To write is to seek luck. Luck animates the smallest part of the Universe: the twinkling of stars is its power, a wildflower its incantation. The heat of life left me; desire no longer had an object ... I was happy to be the plaything of luck' (Bataille 2004: 53). The sensual and sexual nature of writing is clear, as are all submissive relations to art we see, from our ecstasy at Bernini's St Teresa's ecstasy in the infinite unknowability of baroque folds reflecting baroque desire, to the Stendhal Syndrome – dizziness supposedly experienced by people experiencing great beauty. But if we attempt to construct (without structure) our queer selves as expressive art objects, all we ask is that our power opens up the world rather than closing it down in the too human massacre of nature that operations of signification masquerading as truth perpetuate, no matter how well meant when addressing nonhuman animals or minoritarians. Where Kristeva states 'The act of questioning is present in artistic experience, in rejection and renewal of old codes of representation staged in painting, music or poetry' (2002: 121), we acknowledge that, as unresponsive, questions do not, cannot, demand answers. Like the sexual subject which will not respond, taking our cue from Foucault, becoming nonhuman via understanding self as expressive in ways which resonate with art makes us shut up about any compulsion for defining factors of our desires and most importantly, makes no demand on any witness to the art that is self to define itself in order that we may oppose or reflect it. In its revelling, jubilant celebration of being constructed artifice, art demands we exploit and create unlikely relations with nature to become otherwise, not via the content of what we become, but the openings we make for others to become otherwise. Far from sacrificial however, this allows us to live many lives by forsaking the one life of the human subject in our constant malleability. Art which illuminates nothing but affects returns us to the first thing from which we are estranged, our bodies, without signification or subjectification, so that the more we know ourselves as art – as false, as nonhuman, as unnatural natural phenomenon – the more our entire relation with the world is inherently queer.

Nonhuman as Nature

The most immediate indicator of the human is often found in its juxtaposition against nature, defaulting the word human to culture and the word nature to nonhuman animal. This rhetoric justifies the murder and torture of nonhuman animals because they belong to the unconstructed and therefore somehow non-self-aware mechanised operations of nature, while humans belong to the sentient operations of culture, which, through our self-determined construction gives us the right to manipulate what, within this logic, cannot manipulate itself. Even much animal rights work attempts to drag nonhumans up to culture, imposing or demarcating a culture of nonhumans in order to vindicate their right to live only due to the ways they reflect human cultural operations. Nature is seen as a dumb mute accidental performance of phenomenon when it is denigrated as the lesser in the binary of the self-styled science of the human, and when the human discovers 'truths' in nature they are raised to a more noble status due to their becoming manipulatable. This is one problem with versions of posthuman theory that place the cyborg biotech human as the zenith of promises of ultimate self-realisation, where a relationship with nature is sought only to vanquish, reorient or exploit it toward posthuman as hyperhumanist goals. For this reason I prefer the concept of the 'ahuman' to the posthuman (MacCormack 2014) as it includes the natural phenomenon human organisms are in its address to relations, yet also demands the human forsake the more destructive compulsions which reiterate human subjectivity as a pattern of violation of nonhumans. Humans are social, nonhuman animals are natural, the humanist tells us. Yet, this society is what makes us a giant, mindless consuming phenomenon which overlays nature rather than being within the web of relations with nature. The social contract suffocates the natural contract rather than occurring within it. It causes amnesia of nature and demands nature rise to be integrated within the social in order to be acknowledged, verified and utilised. If it is below the social, it does not register and therefore does not count (as a differend). If it registers, it is made to celebrate its often devastating inclusion in the social by being used as host for the parasite who is Man, because it is included, but will never be that which includes it. As Serres writes: 'Man is a stockpile, the strongest and most connected of nature. He is a being everywhere. And bound. According to philosophers of old, men formed a great animal by assembling through a social contract. In the passage from individuals to groups we rose in groups but fell from thought, to brute life, brainless or mechanical, so true is it that in saying "we", publicly, meaning the essence of the public, has never really known what it was saying or thinking: such groups may be superior then, in critical mass, but inferior in the chain of being' (2001: 18).

Demarcating yourself as human adheres you to a community, even when alone, so that the stylised perceived individuality of consumer capitalism is as much a stockpile of social brainless mechanisation as it is the placated mentality of any human society as a collective via failed-communist totalitarianism, the assimilative operations of fascism or other collectives. The solitary human always belongs to this mindset if it persists in defining itself as human. Paradoxically, the human sees commonality in purpose as giving freedom of individuality, where the very being of human makes one's 'right' to do as one pleases to nature, while ethically common notions according to Spinoza are found in the very disjunctures of relations that allow two unlike entities to flourish in relation with one another. Deleuze states:

> In short a common notion is the representation of a composition between two or more bodies, and a unity of this composition ... For when we encounter a body that agrees with ours we experience an affect or feeling of joy-passion, although we do not adequately know what it has in common with us ... (1988: 55, 56)

The commonality between humans as humans means any inter-human relations cannot be defined as queer. Whether via act, object choice, lack of sexuality or any other form of speech or silence about desire, if the source from whence it is emitted is identified as human – that is, someone who fulfils (or attempts to and fails in the case of many minoritarians) the template criteria of the social corpus as a subject belonging to the species human with all of its parasitic and violating impulses – then the desire is human and thus the relation can neither be queer nor (as will be elaborated below) ethical. Of course I am not talking here about bestiality or becoming-animal, but the reconception of the powers and affects which traditional conceptions of the human as social and cultural construct privilege.

> Back to nature then! That means we must add to the exclusively social contract a natural contract of symbiosis and reciprocity in which our relationship with things would set aside mastery and possession in favour of admiring attention, reciprocity, contemplation, and respect; where knowledge would no longer imply property, nor action, mastery ... the parasite takes all and gives nothing; the host gives all and takes nothing. Rights of mastery and property come down to parasitism. Conversely rights of symbiosis are defined by reciprocity; however much nature gives man, man must give that much back to nature, now a legal subject. (Serres 2001: 38)

Nature does not give so that the human can take, nature is never offered the opportunity to consent, and sadly in its grace cannot conceive of what the human has in store for it so often (in the case of many human-nonhuman–animal relations) and it does not recoil from the horrific dissymmetrical hierarchy the human imposes upon the relation until the full horror of that relation is executed. Those humans who seek to abolish such relations, such as abolitionist vegans, are defined persistently as 'humans who believe/propose …', etc. Abolitionist discourse is forced to enunciate what it is within human discourse via the human social contract, which is paradoxical to its primary goal of allowing others (both minoritarian humans and nonhumans) to exist independent of the human contract. The faux benevolence of 'inclusion' means the natural contract remains ignored by those who will not relinquish their parasitism, because the action of inclusion within the human discourse is in reality the reactive force of parasitism masquerading its destructive affects. For the human to become part of the natural contract is a queer operation. It involves forsaking the privilege of human social power, including all degrees of majoritarian to minoritarian, which delimits desire to one between humans as viable objects of desire or facilitators of acts, including one's self as both subject–object and facilitator. In this way the human becomes the ahuman nonhuman. It also opens relations up to the natural contract, a gracious form of desire found in commonality as producing beneficial affects for all parties based on their unknowable specificity, contemplation as being affected by some 'thing' (thing being constituted by its flows of expression, not ontological essence) without intervening or interfering with it, and attention as a patient waiting that makes no demands, nor may even register. These forms of interaction are decidedly queer in that they describe quiet approaches, tentative waitings, nothing of which seeks a result or knows an outcome, and most importantly, exploits in a positive way the unpredictable infinity of potential relations when nothing is defined in advance and all things are appreciated with patient unknowing. If knowledge is mastery and speech is ownership then this relation is the opening out toward the thought of nature, listening to how nature thinks, which is of course also infinite and before and beyond any human syntax. Becoming-ahuman catalyses an openness to a natural contract, which makes other humans ahuman, and thus even in the most traditionally defined relations between two bodies nonhuman queerness flourishes.

Nonhuman Ethics

In reference to the ethical consideration of queering the nonhuman there seem to be two trajectories into which philosophy risks falling – that of fetishisation and that of repudiation. Many feminists have maligned Deleuze and Guattari's becoming-woman for co-opting women in their postmodern adventures and a similar argument could be made for their becoming animal, but this trend of fetishisation of the nonhuman is somewhat redeemed in their attention to fabulated animals rather than real life nonhuman entities – werewolves, packs, demons and such, aligning them more with the nonhuman as art than actual animal lives. Not so the narcissistic assimilation of his cat staring at him naked by Derrida, or Haraway's Oedipal relations with 'companion' species, ignoring the slavery that domestication necessitated and the continuation of meat production that nurturing companion animals fosters, rigorously maintaining speciesist hierarchies. Speciesism continues in contemporary animal studies. Wolfe's work 'uses' animals zoontologically, ironically enunciating 'my assertion [to question species distinction] might seem rather rash or even quaintly lunatic fringe to most scholars and critics' (2003: 1), whilst naming veganism as a form of radical posturing. Contemporary media trends from social media to digital theory assimilate human perceptions of insect hive interactions. Even animal rights in its traditional Singer (1996) incarnation, equivocates reflecting the human with greater integrity of life and liberty. This default position suggests the term nonhuman can refer the human to new ways of augmenting our own existential crisis by rethinking ourselves through taking conveniently supportive human perceptions of nonhuman animals – homogenised as species, denied their singularity – to further our obsession with ourselves, be it in affirmation of superiority or toward alternate understandings of human subjectivity. While the latter is an absolutely necessary project for thinking ethical ecosophical futures (without the use of subjectivity), it seems particularly cruel that we look to the very organisms we enslave and destroy to get us out of the philosophical identity crisis we continue to create for ourselves, rather than seek to unravel the concept of the human in order to open ourselves to the world beyond – beyond language, beyond structure, beyond dialectics and beyond signification. Spinoza states: 'Emulation is the desire of something engendered in us by our conception that others have the same desire' (1957: 68). Thus, any thinking the animal is not to liberate them but to further bend and conform their freedom to our use.

Abolitionism, by contrast, advocates the cessation of thinking the animal at all, as thinking the animal knows and manipulates it. (This does not preclude care, but care without reason, not through what an animal is but *that* it is.) Fabulated nonhumans and natural nonhumans show the human has always been a unique combination of a nature it cannot know and an imagination which has no limit, while humanism obsessively seeks to know nature in order to control it and limit imagination in order to regulate subjectivity through a perception of the concept of 'truth' as a limit of the possible. Queering the nonhuman requires a very careful consideration of how we use nonhuman, because all thought is ultimately use in that it produces material affects via action upon the bodies of others. As we humans are the only species which needs unravelling (and the only species into which we have the right to intervene), we are faced with the limitless energy invigorated in thinking what we already are differently without co-opting anything else.

The nonhuman understood in this way is the difference within the human that is nonhuman, but not like any nonhuman animal individual (and never like a species, a term which should be abolished in ethical considerations of nature). Queering the nonhuman queers the human so all humans become nonhuman – unlike themselves as the selves they perceive themselves to be and unlike the too often destructive values which accompany these. The role of queer is emphasised, as the noun nonhuman is secondary, even tactical, compared to the verb queering, because it privileges relation over being. Ethically this difference in itself is reminiscent of a body without organs, as, according to Spinoza 'the human body is composed of very many parts of different nature, which stand in continual need of varied nourishment, so that the whole body may be equally capable of doing everything that can follow from its own nature' (1957: 132). Spinoza is very clear in this section of the *Ethics* that love, not admiration or hope, are what constitute ethics. 'Thinking' the animal is without love, be it via the robbery of specificity which comes from metaphor or ethology as forms of admiration, or offering reasons why animals 'deserve' a better future through diminished human-generated torture and murder, where hope still relies on the animal proving itself. Abolitionism is love, because it makes us accountable for the expression of a passion – love – without demand for reciprocity or intervention – grace – that leads to leaving nonhuman animals alone by not intervening in their use for any reason.

In *The Way of Love* Irigaray states:

> To suppose Being as the whole of being as ground does not take account of the ground that the relation between human beings represents. This relation does not realise itself as the result of a gathering of human beings, of people for example. It takes place each time between two subjects … The relation between those who are the same and different weaves a groundless ground. It corresponds neither to the abyss nor to nothingness but results from an act of grounding which does not end in any ground. (2002b: 72)

This natural ground reflects Serres' natural contract, where the ground is the queer territory through which the nonhuman emerges, rather than a mapped dialectic social space occupied by two in opposition. Queer ground is natural ground in its capacity for welcoming endless affects and expressions and exploiting the mobilisations these afford, ethically via action – the activity of an organism based on the ways it is affected – and passions – the phenomenon of relations which occur between organisms as they originate outside the organism but affect it nonetheless. There is no need for a fetishised other to find the nonhumans we are within this queer terrain. Rethinking the nature of relation at all is enough to constitute a disempowerment of the human subject as an ethical, activist and experimental action if it seeks to avoid repetition which leads to reinstatement of the category human, in its majoritarian or minoritarian manifestation. Irigaray continues:

> This real, in myself as in the other, contains in itself the possibility of blossoming. Its unfolding, its flowering, do not depend upon the making of something other. In this sense the human remains tied to nature. And when it takes root in History, without fidelity to nature, it alienates there its particularity and the task of producing it as such, among other things for the construction of a present and future History. The human also loses in this the occasion to elaborate in the present its relation with

> the other. And what it considers as the most human of its work then becomes non-human ... which makes the human itself hybrid. (2002b: 121)

An ethical queering of the nonhuman is the act of love that comes from the self no longer understood as human and the other not sought to be understood, belonging to the same species – the 'organism formerly known as human' – but other to itself. Irigaray captures the capacity for nonhuman love and limitless desire without our needing to go outside the human and make another organism accountable for the failures in our own queering imagination. Even her human as hybrid is a hybrid made up of unlikely humans rather than the traditional mythologised animal/human hybrid. It is a chimera of unnameable parts of the human not yet apprehended (and without need to be). This chimera is the parabolic configuration of the fabulated at one end and the natural at the other, but curved so their intimacy is closer than the point at which we believe the self emerges. Our natural animal selves are unbound through openness to affect.

Deleuze states '[In Spinoza] animals are defined less by the abstract notions of genus and species than by a capacity for being affected, by the affections of which they are "capable", by the excitations to which they react within the limits of their capability' (1988: 27). Deleuze is explicit that for Spinoza, morality is a Judgement of God, a sentiment with which Nietzsche and Artaud would agree, while ethics is an ethology which *includes man* as it is a way of thinking all interaction (thought not in an evolutionary sense which would privilege man). This both allows the ethics to remain accountable for any inevitable interaction with nonhuman animals (denying neither human nor nonhuman animal their own unique affects) and refuses a hierarchy of liberty based on claims that some affects are more noble or higher than others. Further Deleuze and Guattari claim '*affects are the becoming inhuman of man*' (Deleuze and Guattari, 1994: 169 original emphasis), precluding nature from morality and the human from ethics should we remain within the realm of the signified subject. Ethics is defined by relation and specific capacities, not forms or species; queer is the ground of love which emphasises the interactivity of organisms defined through their relation, and thus all queer becomings facilitate our becoming-nonhuman.

Conclusion: The Giving Ground

Queer has long been about letting go of opposition, giving up binaries. Nature/Culture, Male/Female, Hetero/Homo, Flesh/Word and myriad other scaffolds of majoritarian humanist signification are challenged by queer theory. Binaries almost always operate isomorphically, where one term fails to fulfil the more desirable status of the other, and the dominant term owes a debt to the oppressed for sustaining its mythological but naturalised power, vindicated through masquerades such as science, truth, language, family, capitalism, church. For queer there is no opposite. The nonhuman has tactical referents – animals which are not human and suffer because they aren't so, but also the ahuman becomings of the human who wishes to repudiate the isomorphic power structures which facilitate all forms of oppression. The nonhuman both does and does not have an opposite. It is no longer animal to man, but it is stood apart from the ideational concept of the human. It is not opposite, however, as to be so would forget or deny the atrocities and not be accountable for the actions perpetuated by systems which value the concept of the human over other life. So becoming nonhuman does not oppose the human – it is indeed the impetus. Unlike the posthuman which, in its most biotech chronocentric fetishistic way hyper-stylises humanist compulsions of immortality, mechanisation, manipulation and exhaustible knowledge, the nonhuman has had enough of humanist directions, and seeks multiple trajectories which acknowledge human life, whatever that means, as part of a constellation of lives to which it must be accountable, while also indulging in the jubilance of the unthought potentialities that letting go of power for grace and love elicits. In a way, the nonhuman is the object queer could never speak, for queer does not define its objects, and the nonhuman does not know its desires. These terms are nonterms which lead to the most important binary that nonhuman queer collapses – the real and the signified. The Cartesian hangover of mind and body has borne out in contemporary society through the loss of the real, however nowhere is this more evidently shown to be a First World capitalist fantasy than in the wholesale murder and torture of nonhuman animals for various 'uses'. No amount of argument, discussion, or 'rights' elaboration can vindicate this.

Speaking about why nonhuman animals should/should not be murdered for food, clothes or whatever use does nothing except perpetuate the denial of the singularity and suffering of the flesh of each animal whose only crime is it cannot speak within human signifying systems. Activism says very little but does an enormous amount physically; it simply stops this use, which is why abolitionism is the only ethical relation we can have with nonhuman animals. Ironically the hurl of the insult 'queer' has, at least for me, been replaced by equivalences based on abolitionism such as 'extremist vegan weirdo', or 'animal terrorist'. All use words to insult a refusal to relate in a way that perpetuates signification over physical activism and false need over the corporeal suffering which should be the focus. Words and their intimacy with logic, reason and other elaborate denial fantasies have become the enemy of physicality. As Guattari states:

> It is the body and all the desires it produces that we wish to liberate from 'foreign' domination. It is 'on that ground' that we wish to 'work' for the liberation of society. There is no boundary between the two elements. I oppress myself inasmuch as that I is the product of a system of oppression that extends to all aspects of living We can no longer allow others to turn our mucous membranes, our skin, all our sensitive area into occupied territory – territory controlled and regimented by others, to which we are forbidden access ... Tirelessly it continues its dirty work of castrating, suppressing torturing, and dividing up our bodies in order to inscribe its laws on our flesh, in order to rivet to our subconscious its mechanisms for reproducing this system of enslavement. (1996: 30–1)

Nowhere is this more viscerally evident than in human treatment of nonhuman animals. While I am not in any way suggesting the liberation of nonhuman animals benefits our liberation and therefore is a reason for it, our becoming nonhuman is certainly *necessary* for any such liberation. Rethinking relations by refusing to allow signification to overwrite flesh has always been part of a queer project, in the pure reduction of sexuality to elements (one, two, many) in a unique relation that is before and beyond language. Queer subjectivity seems anathema, because if a subject is demarcated, its relation seems determined and its sexuality destined. Nonhumanity for humans is to subjectivity what queer is to sexuality – emphatically corporeal, anti-structural, without origin or destination, dependent on imagination, exploitative of unknown potentiality, and based on relations thought differently to ensure the expressivity of all entities their own experimental imagination which then circulates in a constant remapping of the world through the affects of unfamiliar actions and passions. Certainly queer does have a residual concurrence with sexuality or at least non object-oriented desire and pleasure, but for Serres, grace is a form of love and abolitionist nonhuman activism is a form of grace, and certainly love is not excluded from queer desire. The love that incarnates in leaving be is the most ethical form of desire and antagonistic to traditional significations of desiring relations. As nonhumans we can speak of desiring relations with other nonhumans (ourselves included) but we also acknowledge we are inextricable from the world through our actions and affects so nature, nonhuman animals and ecology are an inevitable part of this nonhuman queer. The specificity comes in the qualitative nature of the intensities expressed and the ways these remap the cosmogenic ecology of love.

Bibliography

Artaud, Antonin, 'To be Done with the Judgement of God,' in *Selected Writings*, ed. Susan Sontag, trans. Helen Weaver (Berkeley: University of California Press, 1988).
Bataille, Georges, *Divine Filth: Lost Writings*, trans. Mark Spitzer (London: Creation, 2004).
Deleuze, Gilles, *Nietzsche and Philosophy*, trans. Hugh Tomlinson (London: Continuum, 2006).
———, *Spinoza: Practical Philosophy*, trans. Robert Hurley (San Francisco, CA: City Lights Books, 1988).
Deleuze, Gilles, and Guattari, Félix, *A Thousand Plateaus: Capitalism and Schizophrenia*, trans. Brian Massumi (London: The Athlone Press, 1987).
———, *What is Philosophy?*, trans. Hugh Tomlinson and Graham Burchell (New York: Columbia University Press, 1994).

Foucault, Michel, 'Bodies and Pleasure', trans James A. Steintrager, in Lotringer Sylvère (ed.), *More and Less* (New York: Semiotext(e), 2000).
Guattari, Félix, *Soft Subversions*, trans. David L. Sweet and Chet Wiener (New York: Semiotext(e), 1996).
Irigaray, Luce, *To Speak is Never Neutral*, trans. Gail Schwab (London: Athlone, 2002a).
———, *The Way of Love*, trans. Heidi Bostic and Stephen Pluhacek (London: Continuum, 2002b).
Kristeva, Julia, *Revolt She Said*, trans. Brian O'Keefe (New York: Semiotext(e), 2002).
MacCormack, Patricia, ed., *The Animal Catalyst: Toward Ahuman Theory* (London: Bloomsbury, 2014).
Nietzsche, Friedrich, *On the Genealogy of Morals*, trans. Douglas Smith (London: Penguin, 1996).
Serres, Michel, *The Natural Contract*, trans. Elizabeth MacArthur and William Paulson (Ann Arbor: The University of Michigan Press, 2001).
Singer, Peter, ed., *In Defense of Animals: The Second Wave* (London: Blackwell, 2006).
Spinoza, Baruch, *The Road to Inner Freedom: The Ethics*, trans. Dagobert D. Runes (New York: Philosophical Library, 1957).
Wolfe, Cary, *Animal Rites: American Culture, the Discourse of Species and Posthuman Theory* (Chicago: University of Chicago Press, 2003).

SOLANGE MANCHE

#WeAreTheEarth: Rethinking Ecology and Community: The Case of Humanist Anarchism

The Anthropocene today is both an unavoidable and yet greatly paradoxical reality. It is largely acknowledged as a fact, but at the same time it seems to inject a high dosage of anaesthetic into the body politics. More than ever, the time has come to act. Without wanting to insult already existing initiatives, primarily grassroots, to ameliorate the current *crisis*, the conclusion that is often reached is that this generalised inertia results from the way in which we perceive ourselves and our environment. Hence, the argument goes that the way we experience ourselves in our current position within the world, as human beings, needs to radically change: an ontological shift needs to occur. The excessive drilling and tilling of the earth that current modes of agriculture and resource extraction represent are said to be underpinned by an *ethos* that justifies exploitation. As Rosi Braidotti's work *The Posthuman* (2013) suggests, the Anthropocene is not only a question of 'the human against nature', but is linked to a larger problem of reducing not only our natural habitat, but also people, or groups of people, to a state of slavish submissiveness. Which, in turn, is tightly linked to perceiving someone or something as completely *other* and disconnected to ourselves: the same process of *othering* that nature undergoes. The justifying *ethos* in this case would be based upon dichotomous thinking patterns that declare the superiority of humankind in its opposition to the non-human and the non-thinking or non-rational world. The latter vision, according to Braidotti, is the hallmark of humanism defined by its 'dialectics of self and other' whereby "difference" [is seen] as pejorative' (15). Humanism, in this regard, is the siege of oppression and 'lethal exclusions': a view that is commonly defended in schools of thought that are concerned with the current state of our planet, such as deep ecology, biosiocology, or even the Gaïa Hypothesis (Bookchin *Re-enchanting* 9–10). Undoubtedly, 'the humanistic arrogance of continuing to place Man at the centre of world history' has greatly contributed to the exploitation of the earth for man's benefit (Braidotti 23).

Arguably, however, the turning point does not necessarily, and certainly not exclusively, reside in a humanistic worldview. According to Peter Wagner's interpretation of the prologue to *The Human Condition*, Hannah Arendt locates this shift at the moment humankind was first confronted with images of the earth as a whole, which made it possible to think of our habitat entirely in terms of natural resources: as a thing to exploit (qtd in Wagner 80).[2] Whether we can really state that Arendt views our environmental situation as the effect of 'an earth-born object made by man launched into the universe' is highly doubtful (1957, 1). Wagner's insight, however, historically dislocates the genesis of the justifying *ethos* from the Enlightenment to the mid-twentieth century and asks us to re-evaluate the blame we put upon humanism's supposed anthropocentrism. Indeed, Murray Bookchin points out that 'the Enlighteners [...] were almost one in their commitment to support scientific and technological advances for social purposes – not ideological "hubris" for the purpose of dominating nature. The Enlightenment celebrated human ingenuity and promised to ease labor – with its implicit message of a more participatory politics – not to "subdue" natural forces out of a lust for domination' (*Re-enchanting* 149). To advance this debate, therefore, it would be necessary to undertake a thorough analysis not only of these humanist texts, but also of their reception and the concrete influence of these ideas upon *praxis*. This, however, is unfortunately too ample an endeavour for discussion here.

Without picking sides, or dwelling too long on this argument, this paper will explore the potential of perhaps the most overlooked humanist tradition: anarchism. It will be argued that anarchist humanism, mainly as

---

2   In his work *Progress*, it is unclear what passage he is citing of *The Human Condition*. After having contacted him, he answered: 'my phrase elaborates on this [the discussion in the prologue] interpretatively in the light of the whole approach in *The Human Condition*.'

advocated by Bookchin and his notion of *social ecology*, offers a way to think about the living world that mirrors current scientific research; whereby, it overcomes binary oppositions emerging from its ability to think diversity and community as a precondition for a stable ecology and a free society. Besides presenting how anarchist humanism puts forward a rationale of the living world, which is key to a more sustainable future, I want to go beyond Bookchin's assertion that the problem of the current state of affairs is fundamentally a problem that resides in the hierarchical organisation of social life as such. I will do so by arguing that the increasingly excessive exploitation of the earth and *othering* of animals and the environment, at large, is due to what I call *the torture scheme*: the organisation of our society in accordance with values that our neoliberal era upholds. This latter observation will take the argument back to the year 1957, the year Arendt also refers to, and will establish it as the marker of the spread of *torture fetishism*.

When talking about anarchist humanism, the first question that needs to be answered is what anarchism's humanism, or at least its socialist variety, consists of, and how it differs from humanism as presented by anti-humanists. Especially since the new academic tendency of post-anarchism tries to emancipate anarchism from its allegedly archaic understanding of man (Graham 413; *Political* May 55). Very often definitions of anarchism are reduced to etymology. Derived from the ancient Greek, anarchism would signify '*l'absence d'autorité ou de gouvernement*' (Guérin *Anarchisme* 13). The problem with the latter approach is that it completely bypasses how it is even possible for anarchists to be able to think society without hierarchy, which does not mean a society without boundaries, as shall be seen later on in relation to the question of the environment. The reason why anarchists can imagine a society without hierarchy is precisely due to their humanist assertion that 'every [...] human being is competent to manage the affair of society' (Bookchin qtd in May 'Post-Structuralism' 416). Indeed, is not the Anthropocene itself the ultimate indicator of the human capacity to shape their environment in accordance with their intentions? Certainly, the destruction of biodiversity has never been at the top of anyone's agenda, but self-interested accumulation of capital has.

Bookchin's statement that man's 'potentiality for progress, and above all, its capacity for rationality' (*Re-enchanting* 4) makes our species unique, certainly sounds like an appalling idea when considered from an anti-humanist perspective. However, the characteristics that anarchists consider as distinctive are by no means based upon a logic of exclusion, which thus radically opposes itself to the view of humanism that Braidotti depicts. According to Braidotti 'the human of Humanism [...] spells out a systematized standard of recognisability – of Sameness – by which all others can be assessed, regulated and allotted to a designated social location. [...] The human norm stands for normality, normalcy and normativity' (26). Humanism, thus, would function as a 'dialectical scheme of thought, where difference or otherness [play] a constitutive role, marking off the sexualized other (woman), the racialized other (the native) and the naturalized other (animals, the environment or earth)' (27). The human of anarchist Humanism, on the other hand, does not rely upon a static oppositional definition, but upon a definition of *potentiality and development*. Within this framework, or non-framework, it does not, or at least aspires not to, dominate any *others*. On the contrary, building upon Bakunin's assertion that '*le plein développement de toutes les puissances matérielles, intellectuelles et morales qui se trouvent à l'état de facultés latentes en chacun*' (Bakunin 'La Commune' 60) is the definition of liberty as defended by anarchism, it can be clearly stated that all human beings are considered in their *potentiality of becoming*, rather than by their difference in relation to the non-human. Hence, anarchist humanism diametrically opposes itself to the common misreading of Hegel's master–slave dialectics, which interprets it as a Saussurian mechanism of oppositional meaning-giving or binaries. Anarchism, on the other hand, surpasses this need to think in oppositional terms – the need for there to be the non-free (the slave) as to assure the freedom of the happy few (the master) – by dismissing this ultimately very paradoxical construct:

> Je ne suis vraiment libre que lorsque tous les êtres humains qui m'entourent, hommes et femmes, sont également libres. La liberté d'autrui, loin d'être une limite ou la négation de ma liberté, en est au contraire la condition nécessaire et la confirmation. Je ne deviens vraiment libre que par la liberté des autres, de sorte que, plus nombreux sont les hommes libres qui m'entourent, et plus étendue et plus profonde ma liberté. C'est au contraire l'esclavage des hommes qui pose une barrière à ma liberté. (Bakunin 'Dieu' 170-1)

When considering the latter citation, it must be kept in mind that the earlier statement mentioned intellectual powers, or 'rationality' as Bookchin describes it, which should not be understood as some sort of mathematical or scientific intelligence *per se*. Bookchin's rationality is 'a lived rationality that, at its best, fosters cooperation, empathy, a sense of responsibility for the biosphere, and new ideas of community and consociation' (*Re-enchanting* 6). It is precisely because 'human beings differ fundamentally from other lifeforms in their ability to bring meaning and reason to the world [that] they are ethically obliged to develop a fine sense of responsibility to non-human beings and the planet as a whole.' Hence, Bookchin's rationality and his desire to foster the conditions for the deployment of human intellect should be understood to be close to the ambitions of the young Marx, or the Hegelian Marx.[3] With the exception of Bookchin's insistence upon the necessity to avoid all forms of domination, even when theorising revolutionary practices or strategies.[4] As such, Bookchin's rationality can be understood as an ethics seeking to avoid the domination, not only of human others, but also that of nature at large, which he only sees as logical, and thus *rational*, because we are part of the same world.

Viewed through this idea of 'lived rationality', the organisation of our society 'along hierarchical lines of "supremacy" or "inferiority"' (*Social Ecology* 21) makes little sense. It is not only irrational because it is not desirable. It is also irrational because, as Bookchin explains, society and the natural world could function in a different manner. Indeed, here, it is worth mentioning that the question of whether there should be a distinction made between the natural and the non-natural at all is a valid one, as Timothy Morton argues. Rather than arguing for an effacement of boundaries, Bookchin draws a difference between what he calls *first nature*, which can roughly be translated as all development resulting from biological evolution, and *second nature*, which can be summarised as that which relates to human culture. Both aspects of life are hence qualified as being *nature* or *natural*, without resulting in a horizontal understanding of

---

3 A rather common reading or division of the work of Marx I would not like to support. It is here merely used to clarify the argument.
4 The historical disagreement between anarchists and Marxists being the necessity of transfers of power, or the dictatorship of the proletariat.

the living.[5] As nature and man are interdependent and interrelated, trying to subdue the symbiosis we are a part of makes no sense. It is unfortunate to see that this interrelatedness is not yet being fully acknowledged and acted upon – rather it appears to be increasingly the fact that we have a lot more in common with that which we considered to be non-human than we previously might have thought. Chimpanzees, like us, are known to be in need of 'emotional bond[ing]', not just food and warmth (Harari 294). There is growing evidence that they are capable of representational play (McCune and Agayoff) and, arguably, also of cultural transmission to a certain degree (Whiten, Horner, Waal). But perhaps these scientific findings are not really needed to become aware of our interrelatedness with, in these previous examples, the animal world.[6] We only need to think about the numerous diseases we 'share with animal species' or the bacteria that are vital to our own survival (Braidotti 70). Braidotti, hence, reaches the conclusion that 'we need to devise [...] a system of representation that matches the complexity of contemporary non-human animals and their proximity to humans' (Braidotti 70).[7] However, if thinking in terms of proximity is not enough, neither would it be ecologically viable to think in terms of oneness or some planetary goo of wholeness. To do so would be to disregard the way in which balance in nature depends on diversity. As Bookchin notes: 'ecologists have [...] pointed out that the more simplified an ecosystem – as in arctic and desert biomes or in monocultural forms of food cultivation – the more fragile the ecosystem and more prone it is to instability, pest infestations, and possible catastrophe' ('Toward' 161). It is therefore crucial to think in terms of difference, while simultaneously considering the specific characteristics of every lifeform.

This would contribute to a more balanced interplay between all the entities that are the stuff of life. This is the main reason why Bookchin's *social ecology* is based upon 'an ethics of complementarity' (*Social Ecology*

---

5   Or omitting social conditions.
6   Here a link can also between drawn with new discoveries in the neurosciences as discussed by Catherine Malabou's *Ontologie de l'accident*. The plasticity of the brain imitates our environment, whether technological man-made or less shaped by human intervention.
7   Perhaps it is not even necessary to state 'contemporary'.

21). 'In such an ethics, human beings would complement nonhuman beings with their own capacities to produce a richer, creative, and developmental whole – not as a "dominant" species, but as a supportive one.' Overcoming dichotomous thinking is not enough, we need to think in ecological terms. As such, human beings should not be simply animalised, or put on the same footing as any other organism, whether it be a tree or an elephant. This is also why Bookchin's *social ecology* is not technophobic, but embraces human creativity and productivity, as long as it maintains the diversity of the biosphere and tries to be an active part of it. Hence, he is highly in favour of an ethical development of technology. Bookchin's ecologically rational community 'would use the inexhaustible energy capacities of nature – the sun and wind, the tides and waterways, the temperature differentials of the earth and the abundance of hydrogen around us as fuels – to provide the ecocommunity with non-polluting materials or wastes that could be easily recycled' ('Toward' 68).

Even though Bookchin is an anarchist, his *ecocommunity* does not appear to emerge from the mind of a radical revolutionary. The vast majority of people would probably agree that living in greater harmony with our environment, which Bookchin's *social ecology* aims at achieving, is not fundamentally a bad thing. Jonathan Safran Foer's extended study on industrial farming and meat production, for example, does not only show the horror of the United States' cattle industry, but also gives the account of a vegan rancher and those who are actively trying to let animals be animals before going to slaughter.[8] Clearly, some farmers are aware that our current agricultural practices – based upon the initial destruction of life: the idea being to obtain patches of land functioning as blank canvases for man to completely re-organise vegetation upon – are destructive and need to be rethought.[9] Agroecology is yet another demonstration that,

---

8   In this case, harmony would be about giving everyone, including animals, a life worth living. It departs not only from the idea of the needs of the people, or the supposed needs, but also those of the animals.

9   During the well-known jazz festival in the Southern French village of Marciac, *Jazz in Marciac*, for example, farmers organise two weeks of seminars and lectures discussing more sustainable forms of agriculture. This parallel festival promoting biodiversity is called *Paysages in Marciac*.

what Bookchin describes as his *ecocommunity*, is already being lived up to. By trying to understand an ecological area and acting in accordance with its diversity (its rhythm, it could be said), agroecology would be qualified as a very *rational* practice in Bookchin's terms. What we come to see as being even more radical in Bookchin, however, is his reading of *why* we live in the era of the Anthropocene.

According to Bookchin '[t]he notion that man is destined to dominate nature stems from the domination of man by man – and perhaps even earlier, by the domination of woman by man and the domination of the young by the old' ('Toward' 162). This citation indicates that Bookchin recognises the existence of a time during which communities were indeed non-hierarchical, anarchic. Subsequently, he reads them to have developed firstly into patriarchies and gradually crystallising into class society, that is, capitalism. This linear and smooth reading of the history of humanity is easily refutable by pointing out its pastoral idealisation of the past. Nonetheless, Bookchin's understanding of the exploitation of nature being unavoidable in a capitalistic system, capitalism being defined by growth, appears quite plausible and fertile. Building upon Karl Marx's definition of capitalist exchange as an endless ever going-on profit seeking venture, of which the motive is the reproduction of itself (Marx 252–3), an ecologically viable society is impossible: 'a society based on production for the sake of production is inherently anti-ecological and its consequences are a devoured natural world' ('Toward' 180).

Bookchin's understanding of the irreconcilability of capitalism and ecology is not merely based upon its necessity of expansion and its ongoing search for new profitable domains, but is also the effect of capitalism's preconditions for exchange, which are diametrically opposed to the general anarchist perception of what freedom means. As Marx shows in the first chapter of *Capital*, capitalism needs to find a way to exchange inherently different goods by creating a value-system of equivalents. Expressing that a coat is worth fifteen sacks of grain makes these two entities equals. Bookchin sees this as the reduction of the stuff of life to the simplicity of the 'assembly line' ('Toward' 167), not only because this system presupposes the possibility of the complete equality of things, but because it 'brings the rule of equivalence to a historical extreme, [by presupposing that] all men are equal as buyers and sellers – […] in the free market place' ('Toward' 165–6). This deceiving form of freedom, or the freedom of the worker to sell his own labour-power, as Marx would describe it, is incompatible with what Bookchin calls *true freedom* (*Capital* 274). 'True freedom, in effect, is an equality of unequals that does not deny the right to life of those whose powers are failing or less developed than others. […] Now the weak are "equal" to the strong, the poor to the wealthy' ('Toward' 165). Indeed, the general definition of liberty that is defended by anarchists is that it can only emerge from solidarity, from the collective that considers each and everyone's idiosyncratic needs and desires. As Bakunin describes, freedom for anarchists is not a negative understanding of freedom:

> J'entends cette liberté de chacun qui, loin de s'arrêter comme devant une borne devant la liberté d'autrui, y trouve au contraire sa confirmation et son extension à l'infini: la liberté illimitée de chacun par la liberté de tous, la liberté par la solidarité, la liberté dans l'égalité. (61)

When considering this understanding of freedom, it becomes clear how it resonates with Bookchin's *social ecology*. For there to be no domination of the stuff of life, including human beings, and all that constitutes our biosphere, the particularity of all these elements need to be taken into account, as well as their interrelatedness and the whole that they form.

The latter analysis of capitalist mechanisms may give the impression that Bookchin takes us back to the primacy of the base/superstructure argument so prevalent in the Marxist tradition. However, Bookchin does not rigidly uphold the claim that the base shapes the superstructure. The fundamental problem, for him, lies within the social organisation of life in hierarchical terms, which is not exclusively a question of economic organisation. Regardless of his argument that capitalism took hierarchical structures to a pinnacle, he considers domination to be as much a question of certain mind-sets or conviction, without going as far as sketching out a theory of ideology. The reason why we are facing the instability of ecosystems, their increasing degradation, ultimately, 'stems from the domination of man by man' ('Toward' 162). Of course, in an era of advanced capitalism, the domination of man by man is driven by notions of competition and the primacy given to the market: 'the universal antagonism of each against all' (166). As long as our society is driven by the desire for profit, the fear of scarcity, violent competition, and the protection of individual desires to the exclusion of those others, it is impossible 'to harmonize our relationship with the natural world, [as it] presupposes the harmonization of the social world' (167).

Thus, Bookchin's analysis permits us to see the current problem of the Anthropocene not only as a product of humanist arrogance, but of social hierarchy itself. Yet Bookchin, in thinking that the stage of capitalism he described represented the worst form of domination possible, did not conceptualise its difference from neoliberalism. Of course, the debate on the definition of neoliberalism itself, whether we should distinguish it from liberalism at all, or whether neoliberalism and neo-conservatism are two separate rather than one and the same thing, is alive and well.[10] This paper, however, limits itself to David Harvey's understanding of neoliberalism, as it clarifies our own economic self-understanding that Bookchin omits and, which arguably, remains valid today, regardless from the transformations capitalism underwent. Harvey mentions in his *Brief History*, that neoliberalism does not only reduce all social relations to market relations, like capitalistic exchange does, but it literally transforms 'market exchange [into] an "ethics" in itself' (3). Besides the market, I think that there is another type of moral veneration of hierarchical structures, or rather a process, strongly defining our neoliberal era, which does not exclude Harvey's remark, but on the contrary complements it. I call this process *the torture scheme*, a scheme that is well exemplified in the documentary *Your Neighbor's Son: The Making of a Torturer*. Through a series of interviews with young men, the torturers of Greece's former military junta, it shows how they became the torturers through the process of being tortured: blurring the boundaries between victim and criminal. Having lived through unbearable humiliation, pain, and terror, these men arose as the victors of a stringent

---

10 Michel Feher, for example, argued during the *Economies of Existence* conference that today's entrepreneurial ethos is very different from the liberal entrepreneurial ethos, as it is no longer driven by protestant work ethics and honest savings, but that today we entered in an age of credit-worthiness as a prime value of the economic subject.

elimination of the weak and the non-obedient. Their privileged position of the torturer had been legitimised by this rite of passage. Whereas the military junta did not apply this logic of military training to society at large, the year 1957, ten years prior to the Regime of the Colonels in Greece, saw the beginning of the spread of an identical *torture scheme* as the ultimate work ethic. In this year, comically also the year Arendt refers to, Ayn Rand published her magnum opus *Atlas Shrugged*. In this novel, phases of self-torture are seen as necessary rites of passage for the individual to reach financial success. Everyone starts and has the moral obligation, regardless of social background, to start as a dominated subject to become the dominator. The message is clear: we all need to have been exploited and have gone through physical hardships to legitimately reach the top; whereby, everyone, of course, is considered to have equal chances. This is the rite of passage I call the *torture scheme*, or the valorisation of work on steroids. In many sectors, wanting to succeed in today's competitive economy means having to accept unpaid internships and daily additional hours. In London, corporate firms have their own sleeping cabins so that their sleep-deprived-highly educated employees can get a nap during their twenty-four-hour shifts. In France, 'faire des petites nuits' is the rite of passage of all young future lawyers. Subject to jokes and largely defended in the branch, putting oneself through tortuous rituals, can only legitimise the exploitation of the new aspirants. This fetishisation of torture marks a shift away from running life along the lines of the logic of the market, and introduces a new era of barbarous rituals of initiation, of earning one's simple right to make a living in quasi-fascistic fashion.

Coming back to Bookchin's remark that 'ultimately all of our present ecological problems originate in deep-seated social problems' (*Social Ecology* 20), *torture fetishism* makes the exploitation of the earth by man inescapable. Those in positions of power having earned their worth by self-inflicted pain and systematic belittlement by superiors cannot see the suffering of *others,* let alone non-human *others,* as problematic. When putting oneself in a position of submissiveness as some kind of moral achievement and sign of virtue, anyone and anything that does not recognise these values can be righteously oppressed. Because everyone can freely choose to live through a period of hardships, only the individual is responsible for her or his own success. Hence, there is no need for collective responsibility. As society no longer exists, social problems no longer exist. Or, as Margaret Thatcher so beautifully put it: 'there is no such thing as society but only individuals' (qtd in David Harvey 91). Consequently: collective commitment to improve the stability of the biosphere becomes, by definition, impossible.

Perhaps, humanism did contribute to the arrogance of Anthropocentric man, but the humanism of anarchism, undeniably, cannot be criticised as such. Bookchin, by taking the human as a point of departure for his *social ecology*, asks us to clearly consider, not only the biological fact that we are indissociably part of, and interconnected, with nature, whether it be animal-life, plant-life, or simply put the earth as a whole, but he also asks us to take the biosphere's diversity very seriously. Without respecting each and every quality of the ecoregions, we find ourselves in a devastating monoculture. Thus, Bookchin would probably argue that the current environmental and societal problems have more to do with our inability to think excessive amounts of difference, extreme numbers of lines and delimitations, as a precondition for unity. We need to think the individual as well as the collective, in social and ecological terms.

Today, however, we are in an era of ultimate 'equality' governed by the laws of the market. The absence of all boundaries and the refusal to acknowledge distinctions does not simply expose human subjects to voluntary exploitation and obligations to participate in *torture schemes,* but also legitimises the exploitation of life. What disturbs us in dichotomous thinking patterns is not their interdependence, but the constructs of hierarchy that they presuppose and our inability to think beyond them. What we need to achieve is the capacity to consider the social construct that hierarchy is as a possibility of change. We need to build a future that considers the whole as well as the particular. We need to think boundaries in excess, in their abundant and impossibly representational multitude. Consequently, it can be questioned whether the theoretical framework adopted in Braidotti's *The Posthuman*, even if it opposes itself to dichotomous thinking patterns, hence necessarily adopting them, should be re-examined as an effect of the historical reconsideration of the arrogance of humanism.

Bibliography

Arendt, Hannah, 'Prologue,' *The Human Condition* (Chicago: The University of Chicago Press, 1998), 1–7.
Bakunin, Michel, 'La Commune de Paris et la Notion de l'État,' *Entretiens Politiques et Littéraires*, Vol. 29 (1892): 59–70.
———, 'Dieu et l'État,' *Ni Dieu ni Maître*, Vol. 1. Daniel Guérin (Paris: La Découverte, 1965), 169–73.
Bookchin, Murray, *Re-Enchanting Humanity* (New York: Cassell, 1995).
———. *Social Ecology and Communalism*. Oakland, CA: AK Press, 2006. PDF file.
Braidotti, Rosi. The Posthuman. Oxford: Polity Press, 2012. Print.
———. 'Toward an Ecological Society,' *A Documentary History of Libertarian Ideas: The New Anarchism (1974–2012)*, ed. Robert Graham (Montréal: Black Rose Books, 2013), 161–9.
Feher, Michel, 'Rated Agencies: Political Encounters with our Invested Selves,' *Proceedings of the Economies of Existence conference*, 10 June 2017.
Graham, Robert, *A Documentary History of Libertarian Ideas: The New Anarchism (1974–2012)* (Montréal: Black Rose Books, 2013).
Guérin, Daniel, *L'Anarchisme* (Paris: Gallimard, 1965).
Harari, Yuval N., *Sapiens: A Brief History of Humankind* (New York: HarperCollins, 2015).
Harvey, David, *A Brief History of Neoliberalism* (Oxford: Oxford University Press, 2007).
Lyn, Heide, Greenfield, P., and Savage-Rumbaugh, S., 'The development of representational play in chimpanzees and bonobos: evolutionary implications, pretense, and the role of interspecies communication,' *Cognitive Development* 21.3 (2006): 199–213. Web. *Elsevier*. 16 April 2017.
Malabou, Catherine, *L'Ontologie de l'accident. Essai sur la plasticité destructrice* (Paris: Éditions Léo Scheer, coll. 'variations,' 2009).
Marx, Karl, *Capital: A Critique of Political Economy, Volume 1* (London: Penguin Books, 1990).
May, Todd, *The Political Philosophy of Poststructuralist Anarchism* (University Park: Pennsylvania State University Press, 1994).
———. 'Post-Structuralism and Anarchism,' *A Documentary History of Libertarian Ideas: The New Anarchism (1974–2012)*, ed. Robert Graham (Montréal: Black Rose Books, 2013). 413–23.
Morton, Timothy, *Ecology Without Nature: Rethinking Environmental Aesthetics* (Cambridge, MA: Harvard University Press, 2009).

Pedersen, Jørgen Flindt, and Stephensen, Erik, dirs, *Your Neighbor's Son: The Making of a Torturer* [*Din nabos søn or Din nabos soen*]. Prod. Ebbe Preisler, Greece, Denmark, 1981. Documentary.

Whiter, Andrew, Horner, Victoria, and Waal, B. M., 'Conformity to cultural norms of tool use in chimpanzees,' *Nature* 437 (2005): 737–40. Web. *Nature*. 16 April 2017.

BOUBÉ YACOUBA SALIFOU

Je suis Charlie: entre émotion et identité sociopolitique

Notons dans une large mesure que le terrorisme, en plus des dégâts qu'il engendre, constitue en soi une machine productrice de l'émotion. Chaque population touchée par ce fléau développe un sentiment de communauté, de vulnérabilité, d'inquiétude permanente et un sentiment de revanche. Ces quatre caractéristiques expliquent le plus souvent les réactions qui rejettent les cultures ou confessions des terroristes voire les condamnent. C'est dans cette logique que l'on constate de plus en plus une stigmatisation ou bien une lutte contre la possible stigmatisation des communautés. Avec particulièrement l'éclosion de moyens de télécommunication – radios, télévisions, internet – le déchaînement émotionnel ne concerne plus exclusivement la population-victime. Il stimule aussi l'empathie des autres populations partout dans le monde. Ces dernières deviennent ainsi victime virtuelle et subjectives à travers des expressions « NousSommes ». Au-delà des groupes, le déchaînement émotionnel touche les individualités. Ce qui traduit la revendication empathique au singulier: « JeSuis». Cette dernière empathie ne s'oppose pas à la première, au contraire, elle traduit tout simplement l'affirmation subjective et individuelle de l'empathie.

Seulement, l'empathie suite aux attaques terroristes révèle aussi d'autres sphères d'influences des émotions. Nous évoquerons à ce niveau la distanciation que le crime terroriste provoque au cœur d'une communauté confessionnelle et/ou sociopolitique. On constate évidemment la condamnation systématique que font les communautés qui sont liées – objectivement – aux terroristes, mais aussi la distance qui apparaît au sein d'une communauté empathique. Nous faisons allusion ici à l'exemple de la situation du Niger en janvier 2015. En effet, les émeutes du 15 et du 16 janvier ont mis en relief une autre facette de l'enjeu de l'émotion en politique: le rôle de distanciation.

Nous allons dans notre texte aborder cet enjeu de l'émotion en politique, en nous appuyant sur le cas du Niger. Dans une première approche, nous allons effectuer une analyse théorique du rôle de l'émotion dans la constitution et la consolidation d'une nation. Et dans une deuxième approche, nous allons partir de l'exemple de la nation nigérienne afin d'expliciter les émeutes qui ont suivis la manifestation contre les attaques de *Charlie Hebdo* à Paris.

L'émotion dans la construction et la stabilisation du « Nous »

Pour cerner au mieux le contenu significatif de la communauté qui naît à partir des actes terroristes, nous allons nous appesantir sur le processus de formation d'une communauté en générale. L'objectif est de voir en quoi l'émotion suscitée par les actes terroristes favorise-t-elle la formation d'une communauté, virtuelle et éphémère qu'elle soit. En effet, à partir du travail de base effectué par Moscovici sur la constitution des groupes – ethnique, national voire confessionnel – la question de l'émotion reste encore centrale non seulement dans la formation des groupes mais aussi dans la mobilisation des membres dudit groupe. Avec la théorie du noyau central,[11] l'émotion est devenue, tout comme la raison un élément-clé dans la constitution et la consolidation des groupes.

Bien que cela ne soit pas explicite, c'est pourtant l'anthropologie philosophique qui va donner le ton à cette étude de l'émotion en relation avec la politique. Des philosophes comme Husserl, Saint Thomas d'Aquin, Aristote voire Platon ont évoqué la question de la disposition chez l'individu – concept porté par le terme habitus. Ce concept traduit l'ensemble de dispositions naturelles ou acquises par l'humain. C'est en soi le trait d'union entre l'individu et son milieu.

---

11   Patrick Rateau, « L'approche structurale des représentations sociales », dans Nicolas Roussiau, ed., *Psychologie sociale* (Paris: In-Press Editions, 200), 79–88.

Dans la même lancée, Bourdieu va donner une signification particulièrement à ce concept. Celui-ci soutient que l'habitus est une sorte de réservoir dans lequel se trouve enregistré l'ensemble des valeurs sociales. C'est donc dans ce réservoir que l'individu puise de manière consciente et inconsciente les moyens nécessaires pour ses actions. Dans cet esprit, l'habitus apparaît ainsi comme un fil conducteur qui permet d'entrevoir la relation plus ou moins tacite entre le conscient et l'inconscient; entre l'individu et son groupe. C'est en somme une passerelle entre l'individu et son appartenance.

Au-delà du statut d'une simple passerelle, l'habitus constitue aussi un bon levier pour cerner en profondeur le comportement inconscient de l'humain. C'est donc un pan de la psychologie des sociétés qui est ouvert à partir de cette thématique. Dans cette nouvelle démarche, Philippe Braud creuse davantage en interrogeant le travail de Michel Crozier sur l'étude du stratège. À ce niveau il soutient qu'en plus de la simple rationalité, il existe aussi une logique sous-jacente, inconsciente mais efficace qui intervient dans la « logique calculatrice de l'acteur ».[12] Ce qui veut dire qu'en plus de la dimension rationnelle, il existe chez l'individu une dimension irrationnelle qui est plus guidée d'une part par les émotions; d'autre part, par l'ensemble des valeurs sociales et culturelles. L'humain se trouve dans ce cas dans un maillage de valeurs sociales. Il se construit et se maintient dans ce maillage comme l'écrit Hans-Georg Gadamer: « bien avant que nous accédions à la compréhension de nous-mêmes par la réflexion, sur le passé, nous nous comprenons de manière spontanée dans la famille, la société et l'État où nous vivons ».[13]

Cette intrication de l'humain au sein du réseau des valeurs sociales se manifeste par la relation qui existe entre l'humain et le symbole social. C'est effectivement ce dernier qui permet, selon Braud, de mieux décrypter le rôle de l'émotion dans le champ sociopolitique. Par émotion, il ne faut pas seulement entendre l'expression d'une forte intensité d'affect, l'émotion – comme le soutient Braud – constitue un ensemble complexe qui est socialement et culturellement entretenu et travaillé. C'est donc toute une rationalité à part entière qui est perçu à travers cette question d'émotion.

12 Philippe Braud, *L'émotion en politique* (Paris: Presses de la Fondation nationale des sciences politiques, 1996), p. 55.
13 Hans-Georg Gadamer, *Vérité et méthode, les grandes lignes d'une herméneutique philosophique* (Paris: Seuil, 1996), p. 298.

Dans la même suite de lectures, Daniel Goleman[14] soutient que l'émotion est en soi une véritable intelligence. En rupture avec les conceptions traditionnelles, chez Goleman, l'émotion occupe une double place dans la nature humaine. Elle est une intelligence à part entière, tout comme elle est un stimulateur d'action. Dans sa dimension d'intelligence, l'émotion favorise dans la plupart du temps l'intégration, la formation et le maintien durable d'un groupe. Cette double nature de l'émotion montre que celle-ci est un facteur stabilisateur d'une société tout comme elle est porteuse du changement. Concernant la question de la stabilisation, notons que l'émotion traduit le sentiment d'attachement de l'humain vis-à-vis de certaines valeurs sociales. Particulièrement les valeurs religieuses, historiques, culturelles pour ne citer que celles-là. Et c'est dans cette lancée que l'émotion apparaît comme l'élément indispensable pour la construction d'une nation, d'une communauté, etc.

Toujours dans son rôle stabilisateur, l'émotion consolide la communauté en favorisant la dialectique du « Nous » et « Eux ». Comme le soutient Carl Schmitt, la constitution d'un groupe s'effectue toujours dans la distinction des membres appartenant au groupe et ceux qui sont extérieurs voire s'opposent à la communauté. C'est donc sur la base d'une frontière et dans une relation exclusive que ces groupes se forgent et se consolident.

L'émotion comme un pan d'une nation

Si l'émotion constitue – comme le soutient Braud – l'élément stabilisateur d'une communauté, il est important aussi de noter que ce rôle ne se limite pas seulement à une communauté restreinte. Au contraire, le sentiment qui nourrit l'appartenance est aussi à la base de la constitution d'une nation. Pour rappel, deux conceptions majeures ont servi de trame dans le débat sur le concept de nation. Un courant qui conçoit la nation comme une entité objective c'est-à-dire, qu'elle existe au-delà du choix individuel

---

14   Daniel Goleman, *L'intelligence émotionnelle: accepter ses émotions pour développer une intelligence nouvelle*, T1 (Paris: Robert Laffont, 1997), p. 424.

et s'impose au individualités par le poids de la culture et de l'histoire. C'est avec Fichte[15] – dans la continuité de Herder – que cette conception de la nation va prendre son élan. L'histoire, la culture et la langue constituent le socle à partir duquel germe une nation, donc un Etat. A l'opposé, le concept de nation est aussi perçu comme étant un plébiscite quotidien.[16] En toile de fond de ce positionnement conceptuel, on constate une interaction exclusive entre la pensée d'une société d'homme libre de toute contrainte historique, culturelle voire même géographique d'une part, d'autre part, une pensée qui fait de l'humain un être déterminé par son héritage socioculturel et historique. C'est donc une opposition entre le choix et le non-choix, le particulier et l'universel.

Seulement, ce débat autour du concept de nation – au-delà de la divergence – s'effectue sur un fond commun. En effet, l'esprit de tous ces beaux discours vise la mise en commun des hommes. Que cela soit par le canal de l'héritage ou bien par celui du choix individuel. C'est donc la question de l'appartenance qui est en jeu. Question dans laquelle s'affrontent les deux approches que nous venons de souligner. Il peut paraître certes paradoxal de penser à une idée de convergence entre ces deux approches. Pourtant, à regarder de plus près, appartenir à une nation ne se limite pas exclusivement à une simple idée d'héritage tout comme elle ne se limite pas à celle d'un choix individuel. Elle est aussi un sentiment partagé, ce qui veut dire que derrière cette question d'appartenance se situe aussi celle de l'affect. C'est en réalité à partir du sentiment d'appartenance à la nation que se justifie l'argument de l'héritage tout comme celui du choix. Naître des parents français n'exclut pas de parler et de vivre comme un Anglais. On constate alors que les deux conceptions convergent vers l'attachement aux croyances comme étant la voie d'appartenir. On ne force pas quelqu'un à devenir un citoyen d'une nation, au contraire, il l'intègre en intériorisant les symboles fondateurs et stabilisateurs de cette nation. C'est donc faire sienne la représentation du monde que fait un peuple particulier. Que cela soit un

15 J. G. Fichte, *Discours à la Nation Allemande*, trad. S. Jankélévitch (Paris: Montaigne, 1975).
16 Cf. Moussa Hamidou Talibi, « Dikko Harakoye, Déesse de l'amour et mère unificatrice du Sahel », *Ethiopiques* 84 (2010), <http://ethiopiques.refer.sn/spip.php?article1690>, page consulté le 14 décembre 2018.

héritage ou bien une acquisition. C'est aussi ressentir, au plus profond de soi, toute profanation des symboles de cette nation. Mais, faut-il le préciser, cette intériorisation ne se fait pas exclusivement de manière rationnelle. Elle s'effectue, en plus, de manière inconsciente.

Décryptage du noyau central de la nation nigérienne

À partir de cette approche théorique, nous allons maintenant aborder de manière pratique la relation entre le noyau central et la nation – en prenant l'exemple du Niger. La constitution de la nation nigérienne ne se limite pas exclusivement à la simple valeur républicaine. La religion reste et demeure présente à tous les niveaux sociopolitiques. Certes, l'islam est la religion prépondérante, mais force est de constater que d'autres cultes et formes de représentations coexistent avec les valeurs précitées. C'est avec des auteurs comme Talibi et Namaiwa que cette question a été abordée de manière limpide. Ces auteurs soutiennent que la société nigérienne est fondamentalement constituée d'une représentation à plusieurs strates. Dans son étude sur le culte Songhay, Talibi,[17] dans le même sillage que Rouch, théorise la légende de Dikko[18] – qui incarne l'unité dans la diversité. Cette même démarche a été effectué par Boubé Namaiwa[19] – dans son étude sur les représentations sociales de l'Arewa.

Ces auteurs mettent en relief la substance du noyau central de la représentation populaire au Niger. En plus de la diversité ethnique, c'est aussi l'unité de la pluralité cultuelle et culturelle qui est mise en exergue. Trois composantes montrent cet état de fait. Dans un premier temps, il y a les divinités locales à l'image de *Kirey*, *Dongo*, *Haoussakoye* et *Moussa* – qui incarnent le culte traditionnel. Ensuite, il y a des divinités comme Serki et

---

17   Ibid.
18   Jean Rouch dans ouvrage intitulé *La religion et la magie songhay* (Bruxelles: Éd. de l'Université de Bruxelles, 1989), pp. 58–62.
19   Boubé Namaiwa, « Croyances, Ethnies et Identité au Sahel: Du multiple à l'Un », *Ethiopiques* n° 90 (2013), <http://ethiopiques.refer.sn/spip.php?article1862>.

Alfaga/Mallam Alhaji, qui incarnent le culte musulman. Enfin, il y a les Hawka[20] – Istanbula, Kommandan-Mugu, etc. – qui sont les divinités de la colonisation européenne. C'est particulièrement le mythe des Hawka qui va mettre en exergue la dimension historique et sociopolitique de cette représentation. Jean Rouch[21] en fait, effectivement, une généalogie de la naissance et de l'intégration de ce dernier mythe dans la mythologie générale en Afrique de l'ouest – spécifiquement au Niger. Il montre avec clarté la relation entre ces cultes et l'organisation sociopolitique et historique. Ce qui traduit la correspondance entre ces trois catégories de divinités et les trois types de valeurs sociopolitiques. Et ces trois valeurs règlent quotidiennement le mode de vie des nigériens. Il y a dans cet esprit la coexistence des lois traditionnelles, des lois islamiques et des lois européennes – chrétiennes et républicaines. Le noyau central est ainsi triptyque au Niger.

En plus de ce noyau central, la nation nigérienne s'est constituée à partir d'un « Nous » colonisé. C'est un pays qui naît non seulement sur les cendres de la colonisation française en Afrique, mais aussi en intégrant plusieurs communautés qui vivent dans des structures sociopolitiques différentes. En ce sens, on trouve les membres de la même communauté de part et d'autre des frontières: Touaregs entre le Niger, le Mali, le Burkina Faso, la Lybie et l'Algérie; les Haoussas entre le Niger et le Nigéria; les Songhays entre le Niger, le Benin et le Mali, pour ne citer que ceux-là. Cette répartition de la population n'est pas sans véhiculer les représentations sociales au-delà des frontières du Niger. En ce sens, le « monde » que véhicule ce noyau central dépasse les frontières du pays.

Aussi, faut-il le souligner, le « Nous » des pays colonisés – en général – est le plus souvent bâti à partir de la distinction entre les colonisés et les colonisateurs/ entre colonie et métropole. Dans cette logique, la constitution du « Nous » Nigérien s'est effectué dans la distanciation voire l'opposition – pacifique et souvent violente – à l'égard de l'ancienne métropole notamment la France – qui constitue une sorte de « Eux ». Une distanciation qui reste sur le fond d'appartenance puisque les valeurs

---

20 Le Hawka est un culte de possession qui est né dans la zone à cheval entre le Maouri et Filingué au Niger au environ de 1926. Ce mouvement représente la colonisation dans sa puissance du feu et militaire.
21 Jean Rouch, op. cit., pp. 80–3.

républicaines du Niger sont un héritage de la France tout comme la langue, la structuration administrative pour ne citer que ceux-là.

En nous appuyant sur ces représentations culturelles et le statut du Niger, on constate de façon manifeste les deux dimensions de l'émotion – comme nous venons de l'évoquer ci-dessus. La première dimension réside dans le rôle de stabilisateur de la nation. Car, ces représentations transcendent non seulement les communautés ethniques, mais aussi elles constituent l'élément-clé de l'inconscient collectif. Quant à la deuxième dimension, elle oriente vers l'existence d'une distanciation latente. Celle-ci peut être tout simplement une réaction face à l'étrangeté, tout comme elle peut contenir le rejet pure et simple de cette étrangeté. Et de manière générale, c'est cette dimension de l'émotion qui nourrit et entretient le sentiment de la xénophobie, du racisme, etc. D'autant plus qu'elle prédispose les membres de la communauté accueillante le mépris et le dégout d'une communauté accueillie. Et Jean Rouch évoque de manière tacite cet état de fait lorsqu'il fait la peinture de la relation entre l'administration coloniale et le culte Hawka d'une part, puis, le même Hawka et les prêtres du culte traditionnel d'autre part. En effet, l'administration coloniale de l'époque rejette catégoriquement ce nouveau culte – en sanctionnant physiquement les adeptes. Alors que les prêtres traditionnels refusent d'accueillir ce culte dans leur panthéon. Il y a donc une double réticence. Une première réticence qui ne reconnaît pas l'élévation du culte au statut de l'administration coloniale et une deuxième qui ferme la porte au colonisateur.

En toile de fond de cette double réticence, on constate déjà qu'il y a non seulement un rejet du colonisateur, mais aussi un rejet du colonisé. De ce fait, la lutte entre ces deux catégories de communauté continue jusque dans les représentations. C'est surtout par le biais de l'émotion que cette double exclusion va se manifester.

L'acte terroriste comme stimulateur de l'émotion déstabilisatrice

C'est en lien avec le terrorisme que nous allons mettre en exergue l'ambivalence de l'émotion. Nous avons vu dans la première partie que l'émotion constitue un élément stabilisateur du « Nous » tout comme elle

Je suis Charlie: entre émotion et identité sociopolitique

permet de distinguer le « Nous » des « Eux ». Cette fois-ci, nous allons voir comment l'émotion peut ébranler le « Nous », voire le déstabiliser, en accentuant l'opposition du « Nous » à « Eux ».

Mobilisons Paul Ricœur pour commencer. En s'intéressant à la dimension individuelle, Ricœur montre comment l'émotion est souvent l'instigatrice d'un changement radical de l'attitude humaine. En s'appuyant sur des auteurs comme Pierre Janet, René Dejean et Pradines, effectivement, Paul Ricœur[22] souligne que l'émotion se manifeste par son caractère dérégulant. Et cela, à l'opposé du sentiment ordinaire. Non seulement elle échappe au contrôle de la conscience, mais aussi l'émotion constitue un élément-clé pour l'involontaire, c'est-à-dire les instincts primaires de l'humain. Sans oublier que cette particularité de l'émotion ne se limite pas seulement à une simple réaction interne. Elle se manifeste aussi par l'agissement de l'individu tout en « habillant » le but que poursuit celui-ci. Nous voyons couramment des personnes, sous émotion, fuir, frapper, pleurer, crier, etc. L'émotion, dans cet esprit, agite l'humain et l'entraine à l'action, parfois, contre son gré. Cet état de fait ne se confine pas exclusivement au niveau de l'individu. Il s'observe aussi au sein des groupes, des communautés, des sociétés voire des nations. Nous observons les pleurs et les coups de colère des supporteurs des équipes de football, les joies des partisans d'un candidat victorieux, par exemple.

Dans le cas spécifique des attaques terroristes, l'émotion se déchaine et stimule certaines représentations sociales. En effet, l'amputation, le déchiquètement, la décapitation et la mort constituent le lot des faits que l'on constate après les différentes attaques terroristes. En plus des victimes, la violence terroriste stimule la peur et la désolation dans le cœur des proches, compatriotes voire chaque individu. Le terrorisme devient un stimulateur d'émotion dans la société victime tout comme il provoque une vague d'indignation de part le monde.

À lire sous l'angle fonctionnaliste, on ne se rend à l'évidence que l'acte terroriste engendre deux réactions différentes mais qui restent intimement

---

22 Paul Ricœur, *Philosophie de la volonté, 1. Le Volontaire et l'involontaire* (Paris: Points, 2009), pp. 314–21.

liées. Comme l'a si bien montré Merton,[23] dans chaque pratique au sein d'une société donnée, il est important de considérer la dimension manifeste et la dimension latente. Dans ce cas d'espèce, il est clair que le terrorisme suscite l'effroi dans une société victime tout comme dans la communauté virtuelle – qui est portée par les masses médias. Il engendre aussi la formation d'une communauté physique et virtuelle à travers le globe.

À poser un regard sur les faits, on se rend à l'évidence que chaque attaque terroriste est perçue comme étant un coup porté à la république. Ce qui sous-entend qu'en plus des victimes physiques, c'est le symbole de toute une nation qui est touché. Ce symbole est celui de la liberté, de la démocratie et de la dignité humaine. C'est en somme le registre de l'émotion qui est touché. Et l'exemple de *Charlie Hebdo* le 7 janvier 2015 illustre à perfection cette attaque symbolique. En ce sens, la mobilisation faite, en France et sur les réseaux sociaux, est certes une compassion pour les victimes mais aussi une réaffirmation de l'adhésion des concernés aux symboles précités. Dans cette logique, la revendication « Nous Sommes/Je Suis » est en soi la supplantation de l'appartenance symbolique à une nation par le sentiment d'appartenance à une communauté.

A l'arrière-plan de cette appartenance se situe la constitution d'une communauté subjective. Une communauté qui est essentiellement basée sur l'émotion, mais dont une partie du noyau central reste déstructurée. En se référant aux attentats du 11 septembre 2001, Luminet montre comment deux tours s'écroulent avec les croyances d'une nation entière. La peur – qui est engendrée par l'attaque terroriste – entraine un affaissement de la structure sociopolitique en suscitant l'angoisse, le sentiment de fragilité et une incertitude dans l'avenir. Et avec la métastase des attaques terroristes, c'est progressivement les croyances qui s'affaissent les unes après les autres dans le monde. Elle crée ainsi un sentiment de vulnérabilité, de méfiance dans chaque pays, sur chaque continent. Dans cet esprit, l'émotion apparaît à ce niveau comme étant un danger pour la consolidation de la paix et la stabilité de chaque pays.

---

23 Robert K. Merton, *Éléments de théorie et de méthode sociologique* (Paris: Plon, 1965), pp. 112–13.

Dans le même sillage que le 11 septembre, le terrorisme a aussi porté un coup à la conscience collective tout autour du lac-Tchad. Avec le groupe Boko Haram, quatre pays se sont retrouvés face à une tragédie hors normes. La plus sanglante de cette tragédie est la bataille de Baga[24] au Nigéria. Du 3 au 7 janvier 2015, en effet, seize villages et une base militaire ont été décimés. Près de 2000 personnes ont perdu leur vie, ainsi qu'une base militaire est tombée entre les mains des terroristes et des milliers de déplacés.

Cette période de virulence vient s'ajouter à l'angoisse générée par les attaques répétitives du groupe depuis août 2013. Et cela, le long de la frontière entre le Niger et le Nigéria. Dans cet esprit, ce groupe terroriste n'affaisse pas seulement les croyances des Nigérians, mais aussi celles des Nigériens qui partagent plus de 600 km de frontière avec les victimes directes. Dans cette logique, Boko Haram déstructure non seulement le noyau central d'une population transnationale, mais aussi affecte et brise au plus profond une communauté émotionnelle. Il ramène ainsi cette frange de la nation à l'état grégaire de ses représentations et à l'effroyable misère de la réalité – pauvreté, chômage, déscolarisation et ainsi de suite.

À ce choc vient s'ajouter les attaques de *Charlie Hebdo*. Un autre choc face au terrorisme qui froisse une deuxième fois une catégorie de la représentation sociopolitique. Faut-il le rappeler, nous venons de voir qu'effectivement le noyau central de la nation nigérienne contient dans son triptyque une couche des valeurs européennes – incarné par le Hawka. La république en soi est bâtie à partir des valeurs républicaines essentiellement calquées sur celles de la France. En ce sens, attaquer le symbole de la république française, c'est aussi toucher cette couche du noyau central. Dans la même lancée, la virulence de Boko Haram est dirigée non seulement vers les membres physiques de la même communauté transnationale – Kanuri par exemple – mais aussi de la même confession: musulmans. C'est donc un double choc que subit cette population. D'une part le symbole physique biologique est visé, mais aussi la deuxième couche du noyau central est visée, notamment l'islam.

---

24 Amnesty International, « Report: Boko Haram Nigeria Massacre » (2015), <https://www.amnesty.org/fr/press-releases/2015/01/nigeria-massacre-possibly-deadliest-boko- haram-s-history>, page consulté le 7 mai 2017.

Finalement, les deux attaques ont tout simplement ébranlé le noyau central de la nation nigérienne. Ni la tradition, ni les valeurs islamiques et les valeurs européennes ne les protègent contre les terroristes. De surcroit, la pauvreté ambiante et le manque d'équipement militaire suppriment le repère de cette population. Puis, la forte visibilité de la « communauté émotionnelle », autour des attaques de *Charlie Hebdo* et la présence des officiels nigériens à la manifestation qui a suivi, ramène cette population au cœur de la dialectique entre le « Nous » et le « Eux » c'est-à-dire, l'ancienne colonie et la métropole. Et au cœur de cette dialectique, on retrouve la manifestation émotionnelle et violente de la réticence – que nous avons initialement mis en relief dans le mythe des Hawka.

Conclusion

L'analyse de la place de l'émotion dans la constitution et la consolidation d'une communauté voire d'une nation constitue, en soi, le moyen idéal pour étudier non seulement celle-ci dans sa structuration, mais aussi d'étudier son interaction avec d'autres nations. En nous appuyant sur la nation nigérienne, nous avons pu cerner et comprendre que le noyau central de cette nation, en plus d'être triptyque, dépasse le territoire physique du pays.

Dans la même démarche, cette étude a mis en relief la double dimension de l'émotion au sein d'une communauté. Dans un premier temps, l'émotion constitue la passerelle qui connecte et maintient durablement la relation entre un individu et son groupe, tout comme la circularité et la consistance du groupe en question. Elle joue donc un rôle de stabilisateur du groupe. Dans un deuxième temps, l'émotion est aussi la base à partir de laquelle un groupe est susceptible de mépriser ou de rejeter complètement un autre groupe. Elle conduit, dans ce cas, à la xénophobie et au racisme. Et l'élément révélateur de cette double dimension de l'émotion est effectivement le choc de la guerre. Et dans un contexte du terrorisme, les attaques de *Charlie Hebdo* et du Nigéria ont bouleversé le Niger – en touchant les symboles clés de son noyau central. Ainsi, la simple phrase – Je suis Charlie – prononcé par un officiel a fait basculer le pays dans une émeute.

Bibliographie

Amnesty International, « Report: Boko Haram Nigeria Massacre » (2015), <https://www.amnesty.org/fr/press-releases/2015/01/nigeria-massacre-possibly-deadliest-boko-haram-s-history>, page consulté le 7 mai 2017.

Boubé Namaiwa, « Croyances, Ethnies et Identité au Sahel: Du multiple à l'Un », *Ethiopiques* n° 90 (2013), <http://ethiopiques.refer.sn/spip.php?article1862>.

Braud, Philippe, *L'émotion en politique* (Paris: Presses de la Fondation nationale des sciences politiques, 1996).

Fichte, J. G., *Discours à la Nation Allemande*, trad. S. Jankélévitch (Paris: Montaigne, 1975).

Hamidou Talibi, Moussa, « Dikko Harakoye, Déesse de l'amour et mère unificatrice du Sahel », *Ethiopiques* 84 (2010), <http://ethiopiques.refer.sn/spip.php?article1690>, page consulté le 14 décembre 2018.

Gadamer, Hans-Georg, *Vérité et méthode, les grandes lignes d'une herméneutique philosophique* (Paris: Seuil, 1996).

Goleman, Daniel, *L'intelligence émotionnelle: accepter ses émotions pour développer une intelligence nouvelle*, T1 (Paris: Robert Laffont, 1997).

Merton, Robert K., *Éléments de théorie et de méthode sociologique* (Paris: Plon, 1965).

Moïsi, Dominique, *La géopolitique de l'émotion* (Paris: Flammarion, 2009).

Rateau, Patrick, « L'approche structurale des représentations sociales », dans Nicolas Roussiau, ed., *Psychologie sociale* (Paris: In-Press Editions, 200), 79–88.

Renan, Ernest, *Qu'est-ce qu'une Nation? et autres essais politique* (Paris: Presses Pocket, 1992).

Ricœur, Paul, *Philosophie de la volonté, 1. Le Volontaire et l'involontaire* (Paris: Points, 2009).

Rouch, Jean, *La religion et la magie songhay* (Bruxelles: Éd. de l'Université de Bruxelles, 1989).

ALEXANDRE LESKANICH

'The metamorphosis of the world into man':[25] The Anthropocene and the Historical Administration of Human Identity

Précis

Today, the human mind requires new administrative strategies to cope with the ecological failure of its world-project. The Anthropocene, an informal categorisation in geologic time characterised by the transformational impacts of human activity, is the latest attempt to comprehend the world. As such, it forms an example of historical administration testifying to the poverty of this world-arrangement; to the lateness of its existence. This chapter therefore proceeds to discuss *administrative strategy* as a means of *comprehension* that aims to compensate for the lack of sense in human affairs; to propose that history forms the most *comprehensive technology* for administering existence hitherto devised, ensuring that the world presents itself as a meaningful historical arrangement; to argue that the Anthropocene is the latest example of *comprehensive historical administration* that ultimately fails to compensate for the inadequacy of the historical situation it aims to comprehend. As an incarcerating *identitary proposition*, the Anthropocene can only detain humanity in a world of its own making, binding it to an already antiquated existence.

---

25 Nietzsche in 'Truth and Lies in a Non-moral Sense' (1873).

Administrative Strategies

Human beings are existentially vulnerable. They must encounter and survive a world of formidable complexity. Indeed, increasingly concentrated in vast metropolises, they must negotiate and manage a world of their own design. Expressed and facilitated through the symbolic system, their enhanced cognitive capacities enable the implementation of *administrative strategies* to manage the world in their own interests. That world, the world anthropogenically engineered, is itself fabricated at the behest of signs and symbols.

Administrative strategies hence work symbolically, conceptually, with words of order or command: that is, with categorisations, classifications, codifications. These evince an organisational, managerial intention. Administrative strategies may well be abstract, ideational, but the behaviours they promote are not.

Administration itself derives from the need for *comprehension*, for understanding. Comprehension is administrative insofar as it rests upon a technical, managerial mode of cognition. Usually this mode seeks to discover in reality a comprehensive order able to explain its phenomena. But actually this order must be symbolically invested in that reality to explain and make it meaningful. It thus *compensates* for the otherwise incomprehensible variety of phenomena in existence. For the environment the mind would otherwise encounter in itself contains no inherent, let alone satisfactorily meaningful, symmetry or arrangement. Rather, as William James argues, to make it make sense, a symbolic order of comprehension must be constructed at the expense of an extensive 'collateral contemporaneity'.[26] 'The human mind', he observes, 'is essentially partial. It can be efficient at all only by *picking out* what to attend to, and ignoring everything else, – by narrowing its point of view.'[27] Condillac likewise affirms this necessity, remarking that 'since our mind is too limited to reflect simultaneously on

---

26 W. James, 'Reflex Action and Theism', in *The Will to Believe and Other Essays in Popular Philosophy* (New York: Longmans, Green & Co., 1923), p. 119.
27 James, 'Great Men and their Environment', in *The Will to Believe*, p. 219.

all the modifications that can belong to it, it is obliged to distinguish them in order to grasp them successively.'²⁸ It thus produces meaning reliably manufactured. Ideally, comprehension would hence ensure that the human mind can make both itself and the world intelligible; that the mind, because it has already invested a symbolic order into it, might discern some sense in its own existence.

But comprehension through the symbolic system, particularly if it aims to be comprehensive, depends on a crucial premise: namely, that the world *is* intelligible to the human mind; that the mind really does possess an affinity with the world it inhabits. Comprehension presumes that mind and world converge in such a way that the former can comprehend the latter. So, for Descartes, the mind of man is *adequate* to the task of knowing the material world because he is created by God and endowed with a capacity for rational inquiry. Moreover, due to God's benevolence, he concludes, the world is so constructed that man is able to know it. And it is precisely this appeal to *identity* which forms one of the fundamental principles of thought. It grounds the premise of intelligibility on which comprehension relies. For the presumption that there exists a relation of conformity, a fundamental congruence between word and object, thought and being, mind and world, is predicated on the *identity principle*. This tautological principle ($A = A$) is 'an expression of self-consciousness, since subjectivity knows itself, becomes real for itself, only by means of the significances through which it duplicates itself, reflects itself, and confirms itself'.²⁹

The identity principle ensures intelligibility because it is tautologous. Tautology, because it is self-referential, *self-same*, ensures intelligibility: 'automatically, it ensures *a priori* that the ideal is adequate to reality, the abstract to the material, the theoretical to the practical – that transcendental order encapsulates behavioural heterogeneity'.³⁰ It derives,

---

28   Condillac, *Essay on the Origin of Human Knowledge*, trans. and ed. H. Aarsleff (Cambridge: Cambridge University Press, 2001), p. 170.
29   M. L. Davies, *Imprisoned by History: Aspects of Historicized Life* (London: Routledge, 2010), p. 60.
30   M. L. Davies, 'The Proper Study of Mankind: Enlightenment and Tautology', in *Thinking About the Enlightenment: Modernity and its Ramifications*, ed. M. L. Davies (London: Routledge, 2016), pp. 230–1.

Davies points out, 'from the Greek: *autos* = self, my self, oneself'. Hence, *to auto* = 'the same'; *tauto-logos* = 'the same word'.[31] For Barthes, 'tautology is this verbal device which consists in defining like by like ... Tautology creates a dead, a motionless world'.[32] 'Tautologies', Steiner further observes, 'can be thought of as strictly formal, as mirror images whose function is one of self-referential definition'.[33] For example, Theresa May resorted to tautology by asserting that 'Brexit means Brexit' after Britain's decision to leave the European Union; unable, presumably, to think of anything else.

Fundamentally, the identity principle consists in the idea that the mind can make the world intelligible because it is congruent with it: the mind possesses an intrinsic capacity to know the world, to identify itself with it. So, for Parmenides, 'the same thing is there for thinking and for being'.[34] Aristotle testifies to the existence of a 'first mover' who guarantees the *a priori* relation of identity between thought and object: 'thought thinks on itself because it shares the nature of the object of thought; for it becomes an object of thought in coming into contact with and thinking its objects, so that thought and object of thought are the same.'[35] For Aquinas, truth is 'conformity, or the adequation of the thing and the intellect'.[36] Bacon remarks that 'the truth of being and the truth of knowing are one, differing no more than the direct beam and the beam reflected'.[37] Locke asserts that we cannot 'talk of knowledge itself, but by the help of those faculties, which

---

31 M. L. Davies, 'The Proper Study of Mankind: Enlightenment and Tautology', in *Thinking About the Enlightenment: Modernity and its Ramifications*, ed. M. L. Davies (London: Routledge, 2016), pp. 230–1.
32 R. Barthes, *Mythologies*, trans. A. Lavers (London: Vintage Books, 2009), pp. 180–1.
33 G. Steiner, 'The Great Tautology', in *No Passion Spent: Essays 1978–1996* (London: Faber and Faber, 1996), p. 351.
34 Parmenides of Elea, *Fragments*, trans. D. Gallop (Toronto: University of Toronto Press, 1984), p. 57.
35 Aristotle, 'Metaphysics', in R. McKeon (ed.), *The Basic Works of Aristotle* (New York: The Modern Library, 2001), 1072b, p. 880.
36 Quoted in A. N. Woznicki, *Being and Order: The Metaphysics of Thomas Aquinas in Historical Perspective* (New York: Peter Lang, 1990), p. 126.
37 F. Bacon, *Bacon's Advancement of Learning and The New Atlantis* (Oxford: Oxford University Press, 1906), p. 32.

are fitted to apprehend even what knowledge is'.[38] To forsake this belief, Davies points out, would require 'doubting the adequacy of the mind to make existence intelligible, of human knowledge to manage the world it itself has created'.[39]

So, orientation in the world relies upon identity as an administrative principle: enabling us to recognise where and what we are, to affirm we are who we say we are. To make things, ideas, and people equivalent, to apportion meaning, to coordinate existence, depends on this self-referential style of thinking. *Identitary propositions* hence offer an illimitable capacity to discern or declare *likenesses* between things: to make them the same, to make them identical. Crucially, they display a human need to identify ourselves in terms we can comprehend, to compose a world we can understand. For example, eschatological narratives employing identitary propositions – that is, placing the individual within an explanatory scheme that evinces a specific purpose in its unfolding – offer insurance against the fluctuations of temporal contingency. These incubate the human mind against an otherwise epistemically mystifying and existentially inhospitable future. So, guaranteeing the existence of intelligibility and meaning in human affairs, identitary propositions lead, theoretically, to orientation in the world insofar as they appear to disclose the propriety of one's place within it. They are cognitive tools against which one's meaning can be measured. You are what [identitary proposition X; e.g. the Anthropocene] says you are.

To recapitulate: strategically, identitary propositions and categorisations display a human species need to affirm our own existence. They also serve to manage or *administer* that existence: functioning to confirm who or what we are, where and when we are, how and why we came to be the way we are. Administration is temporal. It derives from temporality as a fact of existence, hence from a need to manage time itself. But administration – administrative *order* – requires not just identity as a logical principle to recognise whatever exists, to affirm one's own existence, but a

---

38   J. Locke, *An Essay Concerning Human Understanding* (Indianapolis, IN: Hackett Publishing Company, 1996), p. 286.
39   M. L. Davies, 'Cognitive inadequacy: history and the technocratic management of an artificial world', in *Rethinking History: The Journal of Theory and Practise*, Vol. 20, No. 3 (2016), p. 337.

comprehensive *technology* to construct and implement its strategies. Hence the human mind depends upon *historical knowledge*: the most comprehensive technology for managing existence ever devised.

History: An Administrative Technology

Historical knowledge seems to offer that most reassuring of prospects: that a comprehensive order can be identified in the most disparate human actions; perhaps even in the totality of human existence. The injunction to think historically makes this impression difficult to forgo. How otherwise to interpret the explanations historians produce? How do they manage it? Actually, history is a technology for *putting* things in order, for *managing* human existence. Historians, as technicians, produce 'administrative categorisations' designed to arrange whatever happens in terms of what already happened (hence employing the identity principle, e.g. declaring that what happened *then* bears a *likeness* to what happens *now*, and vice versa).[40] The technology of history especially depends upon the construction of *coordinating categories* (e.g. 'period', 'century', 'era', 'epoch', 'age') so that the object of study can be ensconced within delimited temporal parameters, such as the 'Roaring Twenties' or '*La Belle Époque*'.

Such categories and contexts function to indicate the 'coherence of historical time', signalling the intelligibility of the historical events within them.[41] As such, historical knowledge, the work of its functionaries (i.e. the historians who generate and apply its administrative solvents), amounts to a comprehensive effort to supply sense to the world by fabricating the means of making it coherent. To this end,

> [The historian-function] thus constructs familiar types of comprehensive parameters, such as 'periods', 'contexts', 'frameworks', or 'identities'. It ensures the rational

---

40   Davies, 'Cognitive inadequacy', p. 348.
41   M. L. Davies, *How History Works: On the Reconstitution of a Human Science* (London: Routledge, 2016), p. 93.

consequentiality of its accounts by means of a narratological infrastructure of re-assuring sameness projected by categorical coordinators such as 'forces', 'origins', 'processes', 'traditions', and 'turning-points'.[42]

The result, Davies argues, is that

> The world cannot be recognized except in historical terms, in the terms provided by categorical coordinators that preconceive the world as a historical arrangement, as already historicized … For the individual, at the moment of apprehending the world, history always intervenes, history always takes precedence. Resorting by default to categorical coordinators, ordinary language, everyday experience, automatically construes itself in historicized terms.[43]

History is therefore the dominant means of dispensing explanations for whatever happens. Historical categorisations, narratives, and identities intercede as palliatives to the chaos of the world and the indifference of the cosmos, giving us a place of significance, constructing an order in existence. Indeed, in conventional thinking, the very 'fabric' of existence is historical, because it was fabricated by human historical action. Comprehending it hence requires vast quantities of historical knowledge.

Theoretically, historical knowledge would thus function as a map on which a route through reality can be plotted: plotted up to, and hopefully beyond, the present moment. A powerful logic enforces deference to its injunctions. The conclusion almost universally reached – that history takes precedence – is premised on the assumption that to comprehend anything, one must comprehend its history. That is, one must comprehend its history because its history tells you how it came to be the way it is. Likewise, the way it is, is how history made it the way it is. Hence thinking circles back to history in a perpetual loop. One cannot escape the conclusion thus entailed: that our intelligibility, the substance of our situation in the world, must be found in, or derived from, history. After all, thanks to the coordinating categories already projected upon the past, it already 'knows' how what happened, happened.

---

42 Davies, 'Cognitive inadequacy', p. 346.
43 Davies, *How History Works*, p. 92.

In other words, since history is the primary technology for making sense of what happens, and since the world is now seen *through* historical knowledge, it follows that the mind, as part of history, is predisposed to think of itself in historical terms. This fact explains the persistent engagement in social practices and behaviours that affirm history's quasi-metaphysical role. To wit: the constant historical analogies; the endless sites of 'historical memory'; the reams of historical fiction; the parade of historical dramas on television and film; the interminable commemorations, re-enactments, and ceremonies; the insuperable desire, in particular, for historical identity. The mind endlessly seeks historical validation, confirmation, justification, and history never fails to oblige. In such circumstances, no wonder it defers to it.

To recapitulate: the elaboration of historical explanations, as evinced through the proficiency of the academic industry designed to construct them, gives the impression that whatever happens really *can* be made sense of: that historical categories are adequate to the reality they are meant to explain. The human mind requires ways of ensuring its meaning through the establishment of a 'place' for itself by reference to the categorisations of history. History is put first, takes precedence, precisely because it already happened. Because history seems to comprehend everything, because nothing seems to evade it, it dominates. The more history seems to explain, the more incontrovertible it appears. The more incontrovertible it appears, the more it seems to explain. In allowing nothing to escape historical administration, no strategy appears surer of its own success.

The Anthropocene: A Comprehensive Historical Administration

The Anthropocene is now routinely expressed as a pure fact of existence. Besides being the recipient of considerable media attention, it is the subject of a large number of books and articles across a spectrum of academic disciplines. Part of the reason is that the term is indiscriminate (i.e. it encapsulates everything) and, as a consequence, indeterminate (its meaning is unsettled – not least due to the parlous state of its object, the planet). What stands out, however, and in contrast to the preceding epoch of the Holocene, is the human species agent that orientates and grounds it. It automatically situates the human species at the centre of global affairs, apparently promoted through the 'switch from a nature-dominated to a human-dominated global environmental system'.[44] Its object or referent is nothing less than the ontological field of existence, the planet as a whole. It aims to conceptualise a new global condition: the world-historical emergence of a human system of reality, a world terraformed through techno-scientific instrumentation. It posits the consolidation of the human species as a supreme geo-physical force, altering planetary existence at every conceivable level.

Moreover, as an 'epoch', a comprehensive structure of coherence, a geo-historical categorisation, the Anthropocene displays an administrative, *organisational* manoeuvre. At first glance, then, this 'Human Age' would be the final synchronisation of mind and world; confirmation at last of an inextricable bond between thought and being. It would suggest the culmination of that grand project, as Bacon puts it, to enlarge 'the bounds of human empire'.[45] That project aimed at the administration of all things, implemented through the establishment of a global technophere devoted to the advancement of human existence. The technosphere, or 'human empire', constitutes the technologically modified world, built to effectuate 'all things possible'.[46] To give a sense of its scale, its combined weight – comprising the technological infrastructure and waste deposits accrued throughout human existence – has been estimated at 30 trillion tonnes. This 'technomass' would thus exceed the total mass of the biosphere.[47]

---

44 G. Palsson, B. Szerszynski, S. Sörlin, et al., 'Reconceptualizing the "Anthropos" in the Anthropocene: Integrating the social sciences and humanities in global environmental change research', in *Environmental Science and Policy*, Vol. 28 (2013), pp. 3–13.
45 F. Bacon, *Bacon's Advancement of Learning and The New Atlantis* (Oxford: Oxford University Press, 1906), p. 265.
46 Ibid.
47 J. Zalasiewicz, et al., 'Scale and diversity of the physical technosphere: A geological perspective', in *The Anthropocene Review*, Special Issue (2016), pp. 1–14.

In the Anthropocene, humanity technically achieves its conclusive means of self-encounter and self-validation: a world completely mapped, appropriated, and colonised. It becomes a *comprehensive reflection of itself.* This necessitates the human species' technological fusion with the planet, turning it into our extended phenotype. Hannah Arendt describes this fusion, whereby we 'have taken nature into the world as such and obliterated the defensive boundaries between natural elements and the human artifice by which all previous civilizations were hedged in'.[48] So although deposed by Copernicus from the centre of the universe – contra Ptolemaic, geocentric cosmology – and relieved of the idea that we constitute the favoured creation of God by Darwinian evolutionary theory, we again find ourselves re-centred on the planet as its most exclusive lifeform: effecting the most extensive alterations to it of any species in existence, and imposing our own version of intelligent design to which all things must cleave. Forthwith, one might presume a relation of conformity between mind and world, language and object, action and meaning.

In this regard, the Anthropocene elides the category of nature itself: rendering obsolete the bifurcation of nature and human culture, or blind matter and purposeful mind. It postulates the supersession of nature that arises with the invasion of human culture into it. To be sure, this utter separation remains imaginary. But is it any less conceited today to completely re-conceptualise existence in human terms? If nature and culture are no longer 'non-overlapping magisteria' (to re-appropriate a remark Stephen J. Gould once made concerning science and religion), not even co-existent with each other, then they are rendered *one and the same thing.*[49] Hence in the Anthropocene the human species appears to surmount the limitations formerly imposed by nature through its transformative effects on planetary existence: from the physical, to the chemical, to the biological. It encroaches upon and alters biogeochemical systems to an extent hitherto unobserved in other species.

---

48 H. Arendt, 'The Concept of History', in *Between Past and Future: Eight Exercises in Political Thought* (New York: Penguin Books, 2006), p. 60.
49 S. J. Gould, 'Nonoverlapping Magisteria,' *Natural History* 106 (March 1997): 16–22 and 60–2.

But this move exhibits not only the redundancy of nature, since it has been absorbed by the human artifice, but the strange redundancy of the human as a category as well, since being human was that quality formerly defined *against* nature and its objects. Nature was that predictable, expendable background against which what was human could be distinguished. Humans were special precisely because the mutability of their cognition, especially when working in technological co-operation with each other, could exceed or bypass both physiological and environmental constraints – what for other species remained ineliminable obstacles. Now, on the contrary, if everything is anthropogenically colonised, if the ontology of the inhabited world draws its existence from the mind of man, the human has nothing against which it can distinguish itself, or anything in relation to which it could assert its own difference. Disturbingly, in the category of the Anthropocene it's all the *same, human* thing.

This tautological identification of nature and culture in the vocabulary of the Anthropocene derives from the form of the concept itself. Invoking its logical conclusion, an article in *New Scientist* claims that

> as we stride on through the Anthropocene, our default view *has to be* that the manufactured world is *indistinguishable* from the natural world. *All* corners of the planet are *under* human management – *all* that changes is the direction and efficacy of that management. (My italics)[50]

The grammatical coercion is explicit. It implies that in the Anthropocene, there is nothing so different to the human mind that it cannot be subsumed by it or rendered a part of its world. Surely this echoes the tautological conception of human knowledge Socrates attributes to Protagoras, whereby 'man is the measure of all things – of the things that are, that they are; of the things that are not, that they are not'.[51] It verges towards solipsism. So to say that everything and everyone is part of the Anthropocene

---

50 F. Swain, 'London show confirms the natural world is dead. Good riddance,' *New Scientist*, 1 February 2017. Accessed 23 February 2017. <https://www.newscientist.com/article/mg23331110-900-london-show-confirms-the-natural-world-is-dead-good-riddance/>.
51 Plato, *Theaetetus*, trans. R. Waterfield (London: Penguin Books, 1987), p. 30.

is tautological inasmuch as the Anthropocene ensures *a priori* that it couldn't be otherwise.

To recapitulate: as indicated earlier, to orientate itself, the human mind requires a world it can comprehend. But to ensure the world is comprehensible means manufacturing a world made in its own image. Only then, in theory, could reality evince a comprehensive historical order comprehensible to the human mind. Because the human world is manufactured and maintained through the technological infrastructure, the life-support installations, now essential to human existence, and the entities and events that derive from it, can seemingly be classified, systematically arranged, and managed for human convenience. Here, little can thrive in the world that is not subordinate to the human mind. Further, as discussed, administration involves the application of technical procedures designed to comprehend this human world-project. History is a management technology designed to carry out such procedures. It attracts because it provides a stock of administrative strategies (categorical coordinators) that calculate, *identify*, the significance of *any* human being or human action. This technology is now set a new task: to grasp the historical significance of the human world as a whole. Through the Anthropocene it hence appears to attain a new level of comprehension: in identitary terms, what could be more historically comprehensive?

The Failure of Comprehensive Historical Administration

> By its nature, the human mind is indeterminate; hence, when man is sunk in ignorance, he makes himself the measure of the universe.
> — Giambattista Vico, *The New Science*[52]

Does the Anthropocene succeed as a historical administration? Hardly. Contrary to its intention, it reveals the limits of human intelligibility. Certainly, its 'cognitive intention is to produce conceptual sameness', a

---

52   G. Vico, *The New Science*, trans. D. Marsh (London: Penguin Books, 1999), p. 75.

'comprehensive [structure] of meaning for managing the heterogeneity of the world and its contingencies.'[53] But though the Anthropocene might imply a comprehensive 'structure of meaning' – after all, everything in existence reduces to it – what it means itself is the breakdown of historical comprehension. Its own historical circumstances betray it. Indeed, the historically administered world exhibits not the triumphal conquest of humanity, but incriminating evidence of its ecological incompetence. That this incompetence is geologically consequential is of little note: to attain a degree of geo-physical immortality at such cost is simply perverse. Millions of years hence, fossilisable biological deposits as well as plastic, aluminium, carbon and nitrogen isotopes, among other remnants, will form a layer of strata testifying to our former existence – should anyone feel inclined to excavate it. Small comfort indeed.

The breakdown of historical administration, hence of historical comprehension, comes out in the poverty of history as a technology. History, after all, is traditionally employed to retroactively account for human action already performed as well as provide the present with precedents on which it might base its own rationality. In other words, historical comprehension, based upon the identity principle, is supposed to synchronise what was with what is; to identify what is with what was, thereby showcasing the identity principle as the primary means of making human thought and action intelligible. It's supposed to ensure that the human mind can recognise itself in its history, in what history (human action) has produced.

Yet by any measure, history has failed. Human history, though still the inexhaustible 'resource' used to gauge the extent of human meaning, is totally inadequate in the face of its own, unprecedented global outcomes. The current ecological, existential crisis, therefore, by invalidating the ability of the human species to identify its sufficient reason with its historical development, induces what Dipesh Chakrabarty calls 'a sense of the present that disconnects the future from the past by putting such a future *beyond the grasp of historical sensibility*' (my italics).[54] Human

---

53 Davies, 'The proper study of mankind', pp. 235–6.
54 D. Chakrabarty, 'The Climate of History: Four Theses', in *Critical Inquiry*, No. 35 (2009), p. 197.

history, though the dominant technology that provides a semblance of sense to human affairs, is suddenly insufficient: not nearly knowledgeable enough, not nearly comprehensive enough, not nearly capacious enough. Accustomed to operating with a frame of reference (human history) that now seems in geological terms absurdly discrepant in its time-scale, the present situation invalidates the possibility of historical understanding as it has been hitherto conceived. That understanding assumed that human experience was continuous, hence that the past could be used to comprehend the present.

But today this assumption no longer stands scrutiny. The world has travelled beyond the reach of historical comprehension. Its efficacy has been irredeemably compromised by the consequences of human action. The protective carapace of human history has shattered. As Davies realises, 'in the actual redundancy of structures of historical knowledge that used to sustain comprehension and in the compulsive, coercive historicizations that pre-empt any redemptive action, historicized consciousness confronts its own destitute circumstances'.[55] Its unfortunate predicament is that the 'guidance' of '2000 years of history' simply hasn't worked, resulting in the 'apprehension of cognitive inadequacy' previously alleviated by historical knowledge.[56]

Hence, although a triumphal, self-centred interpretation of the Anthropocene is possible, it would be inadvisable to accept it. Actually, the planet in servitude to the whims of the human mind is a disaster zone. Transformed into a waste disposal site, the dumping and seepage of pollutants effect the most conspicuous and deadly wastage of all, that of life itself. Its outstanding feature *is* waste: the atmospheric, oceanic, and terrestrial distribution of toxic matter. Capitalism, specialising in waste production, remains ideologically buttressed by the technocratic diligence of its exploited people. This ideology of human flourishing into which we have been inveigled is consuming itself. Evidently, as Paul Valéry points out, even though the world has been transformed by the mind, the mind has taken us 'where we had no notion of going' – that is, it cannot be foreseen

---

55 Davies, *How History Works*, p. 25.
56 Davies, 'Cognitive inadequacy', p. 338.

how the mind itself might be reconstituted in the future by the unanticipated effects of present action. As he remarks: 'the modern world is being remade in the image of man's mind ... Now the mind is unpredictable, nor can it predict itself ... If then we impose on the human world the ways of the mind, the world becomes just as unpredictable; it takes on the mind's disorder.'[57]

Here technological proficiency masks existential decrepitude. The human mind has produced a world it cannot master: a sphere of such technical complexity that its consequences exceed human prediction or control. Once rationally constructed, it becomes an affront to reason. It grows inimical to human flourishing. Most essentially, it inaugurates the foreclosure of human existence – what it was, what it is, and perhaps most dispiriting of all, what it might otherwise have become. This might sound excessively despondent, if not for a raft of unpleasant evidence. Today, after all, we are everywhere informed that we exist 'in' the Anthropocene: that we have been launched into a new world-historical situation that seems simultaneously to be exiting the scene. A disillusioned species, observing itself decline into the past, may reflect at length on how its world might have been, yet can no longer be; being how it now is, how it oughtn't to be. This arrangement of worldly affairs already looks to supersede itself, to outpace its fatal effects. So the Anthropocene might well herald a new phase of history coming into existence as an old phase recedes irretrievably into the past. But it finds itself already growing older by the second.

Hence this is evidently not an act of emancipation – the flinging off of an oppressive garment and throwing it unceremoniously in the bin – but a painful, bureaucratic procedure. It amounts to a colossal, diagnostic survey, not unlike a medical examination undertaken on the cusp of death. Tallying up losses, calculating outstanding debts, recording symptoms of decline, giving final notice of foreclosure. Later, the obituarist provides a summary of the deceased's life work, their legacy left to posterity. Here historical administration seeks – in its own, inadequate way – 'an accumulation

---

57 P. Valéry, 'Our Destiny and Literature', trans. D. Folliot and J. Matthews, in *The Outlook for Intelligence*, Volume 10 from Bollingen Series XLV, *The Collected Works of Paul Valéry*, ed. J. Matthews (Princeton, NJ: Princeton University Press, 1989), pp. 167 and 176.

of proofs – anything that can serve as evidence of a historical existence'.[58] But always, as usual, too late.

Still, the Anthropocene does aspire to be a comprehensive administrative strategy, a symbolic abstraction from an integrated global object. It would ensure planetary difference is transmogrified into purely human identity: the planet as the comprehensive 'context' in which human action occurs. Hence it would imply a certain uniformity in its conditions of possibility. Presumably, planetary potential would reduce to what prevails in the human self-interest. But what appears expedient to ensure human comprehension (i.e. that we can everywhere encounter ourselves, undisturbed by that which is different to us), seems rather to form an identitary vacuum, without any means of escape from the obligation to identify with what already exists. With what, for the sake of maintaining some form of human identity – some semblance of categorical, existential unity – must *continue* to exist, even at the eventual expense of human existence. In the end, the comprehensive scale of this human context precludes its evasion by dissenting occupants. Ironically, the human mind is forced to identify itself with the impoverishment of its 'epoch', to acquiesce to its planetary imprisonment. No wonder Elon Musk hopes to colonise Mars, to eject himself from this human cage of identity.

Conclusion

Ultimately, instead of a conceptual recrudescence that reconstitutes the conditions of possibility in contemporary culture, the Anthropocene highlights the problem of human intelligibility in an increasingly incomprehensible world. Figuratively, it sets up an outpost in space from which to survey the planet as a whole. But no-one actually inhabits this vast, impersonal, panoptic perspective. This attempt to make existence cohere

---

58 J. Baudrillard, *The Illusion of the End*, trans. C. Turner (Cambridge: Polity Press, 1994), p. 21.

simply collapses identity into the same, human thing. It erases difference altogether. That's why the Anthropocene's administrative ethos can only *affirm* ecological dysfunction, not escape it. Its purpose is merely to manage the planet according to an image of what the planet is *like*: that is, *like* the human mind; that earthly apotheosis of conflict, contradiction and confusion. This requires the strategic diminution and *total identification* of the planet so as to ensure the mind can reconstitute it as a likeness of itself; can, therefore, take ineluctable precedence over it.

Consequently, this chaotic self-image brings historical administration to its most inert, tautological conclusion. This bitter triumph appears to realise the Promethean effort to be that being which stands at the pinnacle of planetary existence: the being who determines the identity and therefore value of every living thing. The Anthropocene would thereby stake an epochal claim on the past, present, and most ominously, the future. It projects a species merely identical with itself, unable to escape the consequences of what it has produced. Here, 'self-encounter through common humanity is affirmed because there is nothing else: there is either humanity – or else nothing'.[59] At last, the human mind finally identifies itself with its world, and each confirms the poverty of the other. With the Anthropocene preempting both present and future within its tautological structure, it leaves its human inhabitants confined to their own, irreparably damaged world-project; facing a diminished existential capacity to live with or escape its consequences.

Bibliography

Arendt, H., 'The Concept of History', in *Between Past and Future: Eight Exercises in Political Thought* (New York: Penguin Books, 2006), pp. 41–90.

Aristotle, 'Metaphysics', in R. McKeon (ed.), *The Basic Works of Aristotle* (New York: The Modern Library, 2001), pp. 681–926.

---

59 Davies, 'The proper study of Mankind', p. 262.

Bacon, F., *Bacon's Advancement of Learning and The New Atlantis* (Oxford: Oxford University Press, 1906).
Barthes, R., *Mythologies*, trans. A. Lavers (London: Vintage Books, 2009).
Baudrillard, J., *The Illusion of the End*, trans. C. Turner (Cambridge: Polity Press, 1994).
Chakrabarty, D., 'The Climate of History: Four Theses', in *Critical Inquiry*, No. 35 (2009), pp. 197–222.
Condillac, *Essay on the Origin of Human Knowledge*, trans. and ed. H. Aarsleff (Cambridge: Cambridge University Press, 2001).
Davies, M. L., 'Cognitive inadequacy: history and the technocratic management of an artificial world', in *Rethinking History: The Journal of Theory and Practise*, Vol. 20, No. 3 (2016), pp. 334–51.
——, *How History Works: On the Reconstitution of a Human Science* (London: Routledge, 2016).
——, *Imprisoned by History: Aspects of Historicized Life* (London: Routledge, 2010).
——, '"The proper study of Mankind": Enlightenment and tautology', in M. L. Davies (ed.), *Thinking about the Enlightenment: Modernity and its Ramifications* (London: Routledge, 2016), pp. 227–69.
James, W., 'Reflex Action and Theism' and 'Great Men and their Environment', in *The Will to Believe and Other Essays in Popular Philosophy* (New York: Longmans, Green & Co., 1912), pp. 111–45; pp. 216–55.
Locke, J., *An Essay Concerning Human Understanding* (Indianapolis, IN: Hackett Publishing Company, 1996).
Palsson, G., Szerszynski, B., Sörlin, S., et al., 'Reconceptualizing the "Anthropos" in the Anthropocene: Integrating the social sciences and humanities in global environmental change research', in *Environmental Science and Policy*, Vol. 28 (2013), pp. 3–13.
Parmenides of Elea, *Fragments*, trans. D. Gallop (Toronto: University of Toronto Press, 1984).
Plato, *Theaetetus*, trans. R. Waterfield (London: Penguin Books, 1987).
Steiner, G., 'The Great Tautology', in *No Passion Spent: Essays 1978–1995* (New Haven, CT: Yale University Press, 1998), pp. 348–61.
Swain, F., 'London show confirms the natural world is dead. Good riddance.' *New Scientist* (online), 1 February 2017. Accessed 8 February 2018. <https://www.newscientist.com/article/mg23331110-900-london-show-confirms-the-natural-world-is-dead-good-riddance/>.
Valéry, P., 'Our Destiny and Literature', trans. D. Folliot and J. Matthews, in *The Outlook for Intelligence*. Volume 10 from Bollingen Series XLV, *The Collected Works of Paul Valéry*, ed. J. Matthews (Princeton, NJ: Princeton University Press, 1989), pp. 167–85.

Vico, G. *The New Science*, trans. D. Marsh (London: Penguin Books, 1999).
Woznicki, A. N., *Being and Order: The Metaphysics of Thomas Aquinas in Historical Perspective* (New York: Peter Lang, 1990).
Zalasiewicz, J., et al., 'Scale and diversity of the physical technosphere: A geological perspective', in *The Anthropocene Review*, Special Issue (2016), pp. 1–14.

JACK COOPEY

Walter Benjamin's Arcades Project as the #NousSommes of Social Media

The world of technology dominates, manipulates and emancipates people through its various forms of employment and modes of operation. The notion of collectivity has been re-formed through digital media and, in turn, what it means to be an individual and an agent has also been reconstituted. This is particularly true in relation to #NousSommes, which I understand as a collective articulation of solidarity in response to trauma. This calls for a re-evaluation of the nature of agency and collectivity. Furthermore, since reality is made 'plastic' by digital media in terms of how causality, community and political intention and action are produced, it thus possesses a twofold relation: not only in terms of how these spheres are constructed but also how they are understood. As academic technology dominates, but also allows us to emancipate hidden repressions, the apocalypse has already taken place. There is no way 'back' from technology, and so if this technological 'mirroring' of events and agencies is found in #NousSommes, how are we to best understand and act in relation to this phenomenon? To combat this technological 'doubling' of reality, this chapter's argument is not just to reject the hidden potentialities that technology and new digital media possess, but to manipulate them in a new dialectical way, and in so doing produce a different result. The use of the #NousSommes hashtag is exemplary in this respect, serving as a political contagion that unites people of different spaces and times into a multiplicity.

If an identity is constituted through words on a media site, it can not only attract many to the cause, but effectively bring people to an event and a collective agency. It is this which makes discourse possible and so raises a new 'level of consciousness' through social media. These technologies build a new community, but one that has become alienated and corrupt solely through its use. A dialectical understanding of how these 'commodities' operate, therefore, will enable us to manipulate them and thus create a different sense of belonging.

This belonging entails a different form of agency that unites technologies to produce subjectivities, events and bodies. This paper shall argue that a new dialectical understanding of what technology produces can be understood as a 'doubling' of alienation from the world and ourselves. And that we can dialecticise a new potential for the emancipation of technology within the realm of social media. Walter Benjamin's *The Arcades Project* (1927) can be used to analyse the contemporary formations of social media and their various, labyrinthine passages of networks, spectacles and political deferment as well as engagement. Esther Leslie's *Overcoming Conformism* (2000) is fundamental to applying Benjamin's technological analyses beyond his context, by also suggesting that Benjamin himself has become fashionable in the academy such that his writings are cited without employing their theoretical insight today, and are considered only in relation to Benjamin's own time.[60]

Social media itself combines both of Benjamin's theses that fascism aestheticises politics and communism politicises art. These virtual platforms of communication and interaction allow for an emancipated spectator to gaze from afar at the arena of politics. Simultaneously, however, they allow for journals and artworks to become politicised and for people to become rallied to a slogan, cause and image, which carries within its kernel a semantic, semiotic, and political contraband. This paper will analyse Benjamin's unfinished fragment; that is his studies of the Parisian arcades at the turn of the twentieth century. We will ask whether Benjamin's combination of the pessimism of the salaried masses and their bewilderment at the detriment of the commodities of the arcades, and his optimism concerning its utopianism in projecting a future to come, can be used fruitfully as a preliminary sketch to understand the contemporary situation of the

---

60 Esther Leslie, *Overcoming Conformism* (London: Pluto, 2000).

arcade and its continuing dialectic. Or what I label the virtual arcades of the mazes of social media. As Benjamin argues:

> From a European perspective, things looked this way: In all areas of production, from the Middle Ages until the beginning of the nineteenth century, the development of technology proceeded at a much slower rate than the development of art. Art could take its time in variously assimilating the technological modes of operation. But the transformation of things that set in around 1800 dictated the tempo to art, and the more breathtaking this tempo became, the more readily the dominion of fashion overspread all fields. Finally, we arrive at the present state of things: the possibility now arises that art will no longer find time to adapt somehow to technological processes. The advertisement is the ruse by which the dream forces itself on industry [G 1,1].[61]

It is precisely this Benjaminian notion of the automation of sociality that is important here. If the 'commodification of things'[62] has enacted a historical mode of alienated experience, in which the technological processes mediating the everyday, collective experience of reality has changed, then this affects the very basis of sociality itself. In the passage above, Benjamin traces the history of technology and the history of art as parallel processes, but ones which operate according to distinct temporalities. In this sense, Benjamin's advertisement can be transposed onto the images and fleeting nature of social media:

> Benjamin's intention from the first, it would seem, was to grasp such diverse material under the general category of signifying the 'primal history' of the nineteenth century. This was something that could be realized only indirectly, through 'cunning': it was not the great men and celebrated events of traditional historiography but rather the 'refuse' and 'detritus' of history, the half-concealed, variegated traces of the daily life of 'the collective;' that was to be the object of study.[63]

Social media, like the apparatus of Benjamin's time structure,[64] alienates our experience of the same reality. And, thus, the two points

---

61 Walter Benjamin, 'Convolute G [Exhibitions, Advertising, Grandville],' in Howard Eiland and Kevin McLaughlin, trans., *The Arcades Project* (Cambridge, MA: Belknap Press, 1999), p. 171.
62 Howard Eiland and Kevin McLaughlin, 'Translator's Foreward', ibid., p. xii.
63 Ibid.
64 Peter Osborne, *The Politics of Time: Modernity and Avant-Garde* (London: Verso, 1995).

of contentions in this paper in relation to Benjamin are the two poles of technology and modernity. They lie next to one another and yet do not quite sit comfortably. Modernity is often conceived as inextricably linked to technology as a consequence of post-Enlightenment 'reason', but also as a distinctive shift in both time and the conception of time itself. In Benjamin's time, a new world of technology was born where automation truly took flight, new arcades of shopping malls, fun fairs and the rise of populist masses took place in a spectral array of new pleasures, sensations, fears and diabolical catastrophes. The various forms of technology transformed not only the ways that subjects interacted with the objects of the world, but it also transformed how subjects related to themselves, and thus how subjectivities formed collectivities. The role of technology, or more precisely how Benjamin viewed these technical objects of metaphysics, was to continuously increase comfort, leisure, pleasure and greater happiness; but, interestingly, Benjamin also witnessed an increased commodification, alienation and reification as a consequence of the employment of these technologies in the new world of the twentieth century.

> In the background of this theory of the historical image, constituent of a historical 'mirror world;' stands the idea of the monad – an idea given its most comprehensive formulation in the pages on origin in the prologue to Benjamin's book on German tragic drama, *Ursprung des deutschen Trauerspiels* (Origin of the German Trauerspiel) – and back of this the doctrine of the reflective medium, in its significance for the object, as expounded in Benjamin's 1919 dissertation, 'Der Begriff der Kunstkritik in der deutschen Romantik' (The Concept of Criticism in German Romanticism). At bottom, a canon of (nonsensuous) similitude rules the conception of the Arcades.[65]

I shall utilise this phenomenal understanding as an allegory for the effect of social media, and its potentiality for resistance and emancipation. Therefore, at this crucial turn in the commodification and alienation of the being of subjectivity, the ways that subjectivities are formed as a result of this alienated technological splicing is radically differentiated. Even at the turn of the twentieth century, in the wake of the arcades described in Benjamin's *Arcades Project*, the selling of dreams, the double-fold spectacle of advertisements, the mass entertainment of popular festivals all inculcate

---

65 Eliand and McLaughlin, 'Translator's Foreward', p. x.

a new form of technological advancement which infest new areas of life. Parts of life that Benjamin saw as sacred were invaded by the profane of capital. Capital became the handmaiden of desire. Through this, we can see that new forms of technologies create new subjectivities, collectivities and their interaction through the medium of technology. I wish to propose that, following Heidegger, there is no destruction of technology or forgetting of technology as such; the apocalypse has already happened as he put it. However by re-examining the context of Benjamin that produced *The Work of Art in the Age of Its Technical Reproduction* (1936), which analyses the double-fold affect of aesthetical reproduction not only on artwork authenticity, but also the social implications of aesthetic resistance,[66] we can glimpse a redemptive future. As Eagleton argues in his work, Benjamin's messianic, fragmentary writing style allows one to disrupt the false continuity of modernity in its increasing commodification. Benjamin's Jewish thought in relation to his messianic understanding of history and *The Critique of Violence* (1921) in relation to understandings of the modern prove fruitful also in analysing how technology and modernity have shifted the meaning of time altogether and its redemption in the past, present and future. Finally, this paper shall outline the various tenets of Benjamin's work in order to demonstrate its potency in understanding the nature of modernity. This sheds light on technology and particularly the modes by which art can redeem us from the alienating present of the technological modernity we inhabit. It is here that we can perhaps find a hope for emancipation, even if only provisionally. It is my hope that Benjamin can be used not only to understand the alienation involved in social media, but also, as its more pessimistic bedfellow, its promise of hope. In the very structure and style of the *Arcades Project*, we witness Benjamin's intention of undoing the alienation of the Arcades by freezing the images and objects of the time. This is precisely so that they can be once again recognised historically.

> Citation and commentary might then be perceived as intersecting at a thousand different angles, setting up vibrations across the epochs of recent history, so as to

[66] Terry Eagleton, *Walter Benjamin, or, Towards a Revolutionary Criticism* (London: NLB, 1981).

effect 'the cracking open of natural teleology!' And all this would unfold through the medium of hints or 'blinks' – a discontinuous presentation deliberately opposed to traditional modes of argument. At any rate, it seems undeniable that despite the informal, epistolary announcements of a 'book' in the works, an *eigentlichen Buch*, tile research project had become an end in itself.[67]

Section 1

In this first section I shall outline the similarities between Benjamin's work and #NousSommes, with regards to the commodifications which make up our historical reality and form our subjectivities. Benjamin's early writings dealing with the concept of experience through Kant's transcendental idealism and his brushings with Nietzsche and the German Romantics bring to the fore the question of the metaphysical and conceptual understandings of what experience constitutes.[68] The work of Buck-Morss is foundational in understanding the roots of Benjamin's understanding of the three-way relation between language, truth and empirical phenomenon. The question of experience for the early Benjamin is central to our analysis. It allows us to see how subjectivities understand the experience of trauma and efforts of technological solidarity; and, thus, how these technologies then not only change our experience of concrete, historical reality but also how we then relate to our understandings of this very reality. In Benjamin's view, the failure of the Kantian project of complete self-understanding as a metaphor for the Enlightenment view requires a theological dimension to be added to its epistemology. This would help resolve the missing fragments which inevitably follow, when outlining a structure of understanding using reason alone. Benjamin then moves into his doctoral dissertation, which involved questions regarding the German Romantics and their involvement with the question of history, as well as what it meant to be in the present in relation to literary

67 Eliand and McLaughlin, 'Translator's Foreward', p. xi.
68 Susan Buck-Morss, *The Origins of Negative Dialectics: Theodor W. Adorno, Walter Benjamin and the Frankfurt Institute* (Hassocks: Harvester Press, 1977).

form. In Benjamin's view, the concept of criticism develops a differing conception of the 'Absolute' which creates a mechanism for immanent criticism, or a form of critique that pertains to an immediately historical past, and yet allows for present artistic innovation and flourishing in our understanding of the present conditions. In *The Origin of German Tragic Drama* (1925), Benjamin extends his allegorical need and belief in a transdisciplinary approach to art which is both at once historical and philosophical in essence. This element of Benjamin's early work, therefore, relates to the concept of immanent criticism as a remedy to the speed and presence of modernity, but also the need for transdisciplinary approaches to the problems of modernity precisely because it has shattered the study of disciplines and their solitary confinement. In addition to this, Benjamin's emphasis on the power of the 'Idea' to represent sensuous truth remains one of the many tasks of philosophy itself. As such, the ways that new technologies might embody ideas and produce a sensible representation possess important implications for our discussion.

In *The One-Way Street* (1928), Benjamin expands his concept of the constellation, which Adorno would slyly adopt, to depict a redemptive future. One in which given the present materials of reality, and their past forms and their combinations, can be used to dialectically imagine a utopian future. In this aspect of Benjamin's thought, we can see the potential of social media to be understood as a form of technics (as used by Bernard Stiegler). In Benjamin's text, the city as conceived by Baudelaire and taken up by the French surrealists is seen as the plague of modernity: the concrete, the streets, the multiple layers of activities and people surrounded by images of images as described in *The Arcades Project*. The dreams and wishes of this pseudo-reality would become the locus of Benjamin's analysis in demonstrating the newly commodified developments of the arcades. I wish to suggest that we can understand these metaphorically as an explanation for the new methods of social media. The Parisian arcades which Benjamin's German towns attempted to imitate with all their catacombs of splendour can be seen as the labyrinthine avenues and psycho-spatial areas of the social websites which have taken their place amongst the spectres which haunt our lives. However, in these haunted spaces of seeming inaction, alienation and distance, I believe social media can be used dialectically to raise consciousness. The very structure of the text by

Benjamin imitates that of the fragmented avenues of the Parisian arcades where thoughts are left unfinished, like passers-by that are lost amongst the things, very similar to the endless, infinite spectacle of social media that promises a totalising vision of the world, yet is constantly fragmented. Having now outlined Benjamin's main trajectories in his work, we can examine how the present technologies relate to his analyses in order to demonstrate a future for emancipation.

Section 2

In this second section, I will examine the contemporary uses of technologies and how this forms subjectivities and collectivities. It is already clear that social media has now been used to express solidarity at traumatic events experienced by others; events that are both local and distant from one's own social sphere. However, as to whether this demonstrates any use for the victims of the trauma, or any socio-political effect is far from clear and highly problematic. Though it may at first appear as a minor context for the demonstration of political action, there may be some potential here; this is particularly true given our discussion of Benjamin's messianic vision of history and the political resistance against the commodification of contemporary capitalism. I will argue in this section that the use of slogans, symbols and phrases on social media acts as a form of advertisement, daguerreotype or image, which Benjamin teaches us is the most dangerous form of violence: the sensuous.[69] Whether it be a text, image, painting or phrase on social media, the essence or form of what is represented is able to represent collectivity, community, political action and technology itself. Indeed, if we take Benjamin seriously in his analysis of the Parisian arcades and the selling of dreams, then there is good ground for suggesting that this commodification and fetishism of ghostly images has continued, if not dialectically increased? If this claim is indeed true, then the further development of this double-fold removal

---

69   David Ferris, *The Cambridge Companion to Walter Benjamin* (Cambridge: Cambridge University Press, 2004).

from the political is increased in the sphere of social media. Just as the arcades distracted the masses from the violence of the outside onto the equally violent spectacles inside the arcades themselves, then social media can be seen as newer and far more complex visions of Benjamin's arcades.

The key aspect of Benjamin's supposed pessimism concerning the commodification of these non-spaces is that he also saw a glimpse of a utopian hope in these arcades themselves for an increasing equality, sustainability of dreams and justice for all. We can understand the representation of otherness in phrases, symbols and slogans as a product of this form of alienation through the technological apparatus. And, yet, they also carry with them a glimpse of action, agency and belonging. Such agency is bound up with every act of solidarity expressed in relation to trauma suffered. It is in this agency, that we can glimpse a new form of dialectic that can counteract the alienating effect on being that technology such as social media has on concrete, historical life. Such a dialectic seeks to produce authentic political consciousness and resistance. The central argument here is that whilst social media represents a newer form of alienated plasticity, or another fold away from the authentic political, concrete phenomena of events of trauma, it also simultaneously represents a new possibility for political resistance as a result. One can imagine Benjamin walking the streets of Paris in the arcades feeling equally disgusted and ethereal, as he watches the commodified lives of the petty bourgeoisie Parisians enter a new phase of alienation, and yet also witnessing a constellation of dreams that coalesce to form a new promise for the future. Perhaps the dreams for a *Proleltkult* or proletariat culture is precisely the essence of social media in which class consciousness is raised through a symbol which expresses an anti-homophobic response, or an anti-terrorism message. It may well be through the effective dissemination of polemics and arguments that political action and agency is enacted.

To conclude, then, it is clear that Benjamin and his analysis of his contemporary period offers an insight into the potentialities and barbarism of the role of social media, particularly in moments of messianic trauma and solidarity. It cannot be denied that technology is here to stay. What Benjamin's work shows us, however, is that in the end it is a question of who is used and who uses these technologies. By organising solidarity in dialectical terms, there is the potential not simply to delimit the realm of technology itself, but to challenge the very structures which create and control these technologies. Indeed, this is the relevance of Benjamin's summary of the *Arcades Project*, capturing both the nature and 'fashion' of social media today and the role of #NousSommes within this:

> These tendencies deflect the imagination (which is given impetus by the new) back upon the primal past. In the dream in which each epoch entertains images of its successor, the latter appears wedded to elements of primal history (*Urgeschichte*) that is, to elements of a classless society. And the experiences of such a society – as stored in the unconscious of the collective engender, through interpenetration with what is new, the utopia that has left its trace in a thousand configurations of life, from enduring edifices to passing fashions.[70]

Bibliography

Benjamin Walter, 'Convolute G [Exhibitions, Advertising, Grandville],' in Howard Eliand and Kevin McLaughlin, trans., *The Arcades Project* (Cambridge, MA: Belknap Press, 1999), 171–203.

———, 'Paris, the Capital of the Nineteenth Century (1935)' in Howard Eliand and Kevin McLaughlin, trans., *The Arcades Project* (Cambridge, MA: Belknap Press, 1999), 3–14.

Buck-Morss, Susan, *The Origins of Negative Dialectics: Theodor W. Adorno, Walter Benjamin and the Frankfurt Institute* (Hassocks: Harvester Press, 1977).

Eagleton, Terry, *Walter Benjamin, or, Towards a Revolutionary Criticism* (London: NLB, 1981).

Eliand, Howard, and McLaughlin, Kevin, 'Translator's foreword' in Howard Eliand and Kevin McLaughlin, trans., *The Arcades Project* (Cambridge, MA: Belknap Press, 1999), ix–xiv.

Ferris, David, ed., *The Cambridge Companion to Walter Benjamin* (Cambridge: Cambridge University Press, 2004).

Leslie, Esther, *Overcoming Conformism* (London: Pluto, 2000).

---

70 Benjamin Walter, 'Paris, the Capital of the Nineteenth Century (1935)' in Howard Eliand and Kevin McLaughlin, trans., *The Arcades Project* (Cambridge, MA: Belknap Press, 1999), pp. 4–5.

MARIE CHABBERT

Liberté, égalité … Totalité ? Décrypter les dangers de *#JeSuis* avec Jean-Luc Nancy

« En 2015, "Je suis Charlie" a été le symbole d'un moment. Aujourd'hui, tout est plus compliqué' » constate le créateur du slogan, Joachim Roncin, trois ans après l'attaque sanglante contre le journal satirique *Charlie Hebdo* (Biseau et al. 2018). Début janvier 2015, quelques jours après l'attentat qui a fait dix-sept morts, 4 millions de personnes avaient défilé dans les rues de toutes les villes de France avec pour bannière trois mots, « Je suis Charlie ». Ce slogan fédérateur, publié 5 millions de fois sur les réseaux sociaux en seulement trois jours, est devenu le symbole d'une union nationale – et internationale – spontanée pour la liberté d'expression et contre l'extrémisme religieux.

Très vite, cependant, des voix se sont élevées contre le slogan « Je suis Charlie », d'abord en provenance des banlieues et de personnalités polémiques telles que Jean-Marie Le Pen, Dieudonné et Tariq Ramadan, puis de manière plus diffuse chez des personnalités jusque là peu critiquées. L'argument mis en avant est toujours le même: celui de la ligne éditoriale de *Charlie Hebdo*, agressive, humiliante et parfois même blasphématoire à l'encontre des religions, en particulier de l'islam. « Je suis mal à l'aise, ce n'est pas de ma faute, c'est dans ma culture » explique l'humoriste Jamel Debbouze, « on peut aller manifester pour défendre la République même si on n'est pas d'accord avec les caricatures » (Biseau et al. 2018).

Une sorte d'hésitation, de gêne, s'est progressivement insinuée dans la supposée unité nationale sous la forme d'une question qui n'est pas sans rappeler l'interrogation existentielle du Hamlet de Shakespeare : « être ou ne pas être » Charlie. Plus précisément, la question est de savoir si l'on peut à la fois « être et ne pas être » Charlie, c'est-à-dire, condamner fermement l'acte terroriste des frère Kouachi et militer pour la liberté d'expression, tout en critiquant la ligne éditoriale de *Charlie Hebdo*.

À cette question, certains ont répondu un oui franc et direct. C'est le cas du sociologue Emmanuel Todd. Dans son étude polémique *Qui est Charlie?*, publiée en mai 2015, Todd affirme « que la condamnation de l'acte terroriste n'impliquait aucunement que l'on divinisât *Charlie Hebdo* » (2015: 15). Bien au contraire, pour Todd, des atteintes répétées envers une religion, telles que celles de *Charlie Hebdo* envers l'islam, « devraient être, quoi qu'en disent les tribunaux, qualifiées d'incitations à la haine religieuse, ethnique et raciale » (2015: 15). D'ailleurs, Todd observe – à tort ou à raison – que, loin de représenter une unité nationale, les personnes mobilisées lors des soutiens publics à *Charlie Hebdo* forment plutôt un bloc homogène fait de classes moyennes blanches, de personnes âgées, et de catholiques de tradition, réunis autour d'une bien-pensance aux accents xénophobes. La parution de *Qui est Charlie?* a suscité une vive polémique.

Pour ses détracteurs, tels l'écrivain et journaliste Maurice Szafran, le postulat de Todd est une « contre-vérité à la limite de la monstruosité éthique » (Szafran 2015). En effet, comme l'affirme Philippe Lançon, rescapé de l'attaque de *Charlie Hebdo*, refuser ainsi de soutenir *Charlie Hebdo* en s'indignant de sa ligne éditoriale n'est autre qu'une « justification sous-jacente à l'acte qui avait été commis, en faisant des frère Kouachi les représentants d'un peuple, d'une population ou d'une communauté opprimés » (AFP 2015). Ces arguments ont été réutilisés à de nombreuses reprises au cours de ces dernières années, lors de débats opposant partisans et détracteurs d'un soutien sans réserve à *Charlie Hebdo*. Parmi les plus violents, reste celui qui a opposé Edwy Plenel, co-fondateur de Mediapart, à la rédaction de *Charlie Hebdo*. Dans une tribune rédigée à l'automne 2017, Plenel a estimé que les héritiers de « l'esprit Charlie », et en particulier la rédaction du journal satirique, « trouvent n'importe quel prétexte, n'importe quelle calomnie, pour en revenir à leur obsession: la guerre aux musulmans, la diabolisation de tout ce qui concerne l'islam » (Askolovitch 2017). Ce à quoi le caricaturiste Riss a répondu que « cette phrase, qui parle de notre journal satirique comme d'une arme de guerre, acquitte déjà ceux qui nous tueront demain » (Riss 2017).

Pour Lançon, Szafran et Riss donc, on ne peut à la fois « être et ne pas être » Charlie. Être Charlie, c'est condamner fermement le terrorisme et militer pour la liberté d'expression, dont celle de *Charlie Hebdo*. À l'inverse, critiquer la ligne éditoriale du journal satirique s'apparente à la critique de la liberté d'expression qui a motivé le passage à l'acte des frères Kouachi. En fait, une telle intransigeance dans le soutien à *Charlie Hebdo* est exigée par la formulation « Je suis Charlie » elle-même. À la différence de la simple démonstration de solidarité que proposent des tournures comme « nous sommes (ensemble) » ou « je suis avec (Charlie) », qui supposent le rapprochement de plusieurs individualités afin de soutenir une tierce personne ou une même cause, la tournure singulière « je suis » appelle, bien que de manière symbolique, une unité d'un degré supérieur, la *fusion* en une identité collective, ici celle, controversée, de *Charlie Hebdo*. La formulation « Je suis » est, en cela, le symbole d'une exigence contemporaine d'unité absolue face au terrorisme, telle que décrite par le sociologue Gérôme Truc *dans* son enquête sur les attentats de New York, de Madrid et de Londres. Truc constate en effet que: « nos réactions aux attentats manifestent l'exacerbation d'un sens du "je", qui nous porte à compatir au sort des victimes sur la base moins d'une commune appartenance que d'une commune singularité » (2016: 324).

Or, si la recherche d'une forme de solidarité entre individus est tout à fait normale et même souhaitable pour de nombreuses raisons, à commencer par le fait que cela facilite la survie et l'épanouissement des individus grâce à leur coopération pour l'accès à la nourriture, au confort, ainsi que dans l'adversité, l'idéal d'une unité *absolue* des êtres humains au sein d'une communauté est en revanche plus contestable. C'est ce que signalait déjà le philosophe Jean-Luc Nancy quelques trente ans avant la création du slogan « Je suis (Charlie) ». Dans *La Communauté désœuvrée* (1986), le philosophe observe que l'idéal d'une « immanence absolue de l'homme à l'homme » (1990a: 14) fascinait déjà bien avant le développement du terrorisme et que celui-ci s'est révélé extrêmement dangereux au cours de l'histoire politique occidentale. Une mise en garde qu'il est important de rappeler aujourd'hui pour mieux comprendre la gêne suscitée par le slogan « Je suis Charlie ».

Ontothéologie: histoire politique et philosophique de l'immanence

Pour Jean-Luc Nancy, cela ne fait aucun doute: la recherche d'une unité toujours plus grande entre les hommes est le moteur principal de l'histoire occidentale. Dans *La Communauté désœuvrée*, Nancy observe qu' « à chaque moment de son histoire, l'Occident s'est ... livré à la ... déploration d'une familiarité, d'une fraternité, d'une convivialité perdues » (1990a: 31). Chaque courant ou régime politique, chaque modèle de société que la modernité occidentale ait connu aurait, selon Nancy, cherché à répondre à un même mythe dit « immanentiste » (1990a: 143): celui de la perte d'un âge d'or, où une forme d'unité originelle régnait entre les hommes. Ainsi, l'histoire politique de l'Occident pourrait être relue « sur fond de communauté perdue – et à retrouver ou à reconstituer » (1990a: 29).

Pour s'en assurer, il suffit de jeter un coup d'œil à notre histoire politique, qui apparaît toute entière dévouée à la promotion d'un idéal d'unité par le sacrifice nécessaire de ce qui lui fait généralement obstacle: la différence. Les différences individuelles sont généralement reconnues comme faisant partie de la nature humaine. Les êtres humains naissent de couleurs et sexes différents, ont des opinions, des croyances et des langues différentes.

Pour la majorité des lecteurs d'aujourd'hui, tout cela va de soi. Cependant, il apparaît qu'atténuer ne serait-ce que la visibilité de certaines de ces différences favorise une *intégration* plus forte des individus au sein d'une communauté toujours plus soudée.[71] Un ressort courant du politique – du moins dans l'histoire occidentale – est donc le sacrifice de la différence au profit d'une plus grande cohésion sociale. Quant à la nature de ce sacrifice, deux stratégies semblent généralement employées au regard des observations de Nancy, stratégies qui ne sont en aucun cas mutuellement exclusives. Afin de promouvoir la *fraternité* entre les hommes, les systèmes politiques tendent à valoriser soit une expérience de la *libération* (qui *expose* la différence pour mieux s'en défaire) soit un idéal d'*égalité* (qui *masque* la différence). Notons ici la proximité d'une telle proposition avec la devise de la République: « Liberté, Égalité, Fraternité » (Nancy 1990a: 30).

Courante dans les sociétés dites « primitives », une première stratégie part du constat que mettre l'unité de la communauté à l'épreuve en laissant les individus libres d'exprimer leurs différences permet, paradoxalement, de renforcer le lien social. C'est le principe des carnavals traditionnels, durant

---

71   Le gouvernement français préfère le terme d'« assimilation », lorsqu'il s'agit de l'intégration de la population immigrée.

lesquels les individus sont libérés des lois et normes qui les maintiennent dans un « droit chemin » préalablement défini et autour duquel est construite la cohésion sociale, de façon à renforcer leur obéissance à ces mêmes normes une fois le carnaval terminé. C'est aussi le principe des rituels sacrificiels, qui exposent une communauté au spectacle de sa propre destruction par le biais du sacrifice d'un de ces membres, considéré comme différent, ce qui aboutit à un renforcement par catharsis de la cohésion sociale.

Dans les deux cas, il s'agit d'exposer la différence pour mieux s'en défaire. Une autre stratégie, plus courante dans les sociétés contemporaines, promeut l'égalité par l'atténuation – plus ou moins marquée – des différences entre individus. Cela peut se faire de manière volontaire: la formulation *#JeSuis*, par exemple, suggère un dépassement volontaire et symbolique des différences individuelles afin de mettre en évidence l'unité face au terrorisme et dans le soutien aux victimes. Le plus souvent, cependant, l'égalité est établie par l'installation d'interdits. Les citoyens sont alors égaux devant la loi. La loi du 15 mars 2004, par exemple, encadre le port de signes religieux dans les écoles, collèges et lycées, de façon à lutter contre les discriminations pouvant naître d'une grande visibilité de la différence religieuse. Selon Nancy, les expériences politiques de l'histoire occidentale participent de l'une ou l'autre de ces deux stratégies et visent donc toutes une unité toujours plus grande entre les hommes, soit en masquant les différences, soit en les exposant pour s'en libérer une fois pour toutes.

Avant d'aller plus loin, il faut alors s'interroger sur ce qui pousse les sociétés à vouloir être toujours plus soudée, à cultiver le mythe d'une unité originelle perdue. Qu'est-ce qui, dans notre manière d'envisager le after monde et l'existence donne son importance ou plutôt son caractère urgent à l'immanence de l'homme à l'homme? Selon Nancy, la réponse à cette question nous est donnée par Martin Heidegger dans ses travaux sur la dimension ontothéologique de la métaphysique. Quelques explications s'imposent. Dans *Identité et Différence*, Heidegger observe que la métaphysique, de ses origines grecques à sa constitution contemporaine, s'intéresse à « ce qu'est l'être en tant qu'être » (1949: 17, je traduis). Cette tournure est en réalité celle d'Aristote, qui souhaitait séparer la métaphysique des autres sciences dites « partielles », c'est à dire qui « découpent à part quelque partie de l'être » (Heidegger 1949: 24, je traduis), comme c'est le cas par exemple de l'arithmétique, qui a pour unique objet les nombres. La métaphysique, au contraire, a pour objet le « fonds commun à tout être comme tel », l'Être des étants donc. Or, il a été estimé que ce dernier est l'être dans sa version la plus pure. L'Être des étants est « l'être le plus haut, qui est au fondement de tout » (Heidegger 1949: 69, je traduis), ce que la théologie chrétienne nommera Dieu. C'est ainsi que, pour Heidegger, la métaphysique est à la fois onto-logie et théo-logie: une ontothéologie.

Dans *Identité et Différence*, le philosophe allemand remarque qu'un tel système de pensée s'accompagne d'un traitement particulier de la différence. Il est en effet indéniable que les étants sont tous différents les uns des autres. Or, comme l'écrit Heidegger, « dans la mesure où la métaphysique pense l'être en tant que tel dans sa totalité, elle présente les étants en fonction de ce qui diffère dans la différence, sans se soucier de la différence en tant que différence » (2006: 76, je traduis).

Si l'on considère qu'il existe une forme absolument pure d'Être, les différences individuelles tendent à être perçues comme autant de déviances par rapport une essence pure et universelle, et non comme un élément indissociable de l'Être. On retrouve là Platon: la métaphysique présente le monde comme une caverne, où les entités que l'on croise ne sont que des ombres, des versions corrompues d'essences qui se trouvent ailleurs, dans le monde supra-sensoriel. Un tel raisonnement en vient naturellement à s'appliquer à l'humanité, dont il y aurait alors une définition universelle et idéale, de laquelle l'homme se serait éloigné à mesure qu'il se différenciait de ses congénères. L'immanence de l'homme à l'homme, favorisée par une intégration toujours plus forte au sein d'une communauté, apparaît donc comme le seul moyen pour une communauté humaine de retrouver son unité, mais aussi sa vérité, perdues. Plus la cohésion sociale est forte, plus l'humanité se rapprocherait de son essence; l'essence de la communauté, c'est-à-dire du politique, étant de fait l'accomplissement de l'essence de l'homme (Nancy 1990a: 15). Ainsi peut s'expliquer l'importance de l'idéal d'unité absolue entre les hommes dans notre histoire politique, profondément marquée par ce qu'Heidegger nomme « la constitution ontothéologique de la métaphysique » (2006: 51, je traduis). En appelant, bien que de manière symbolique, a une fusion en une identité collective, la formulation *#JeSuis* participe de cette onto-théo-logique millénaire.

Entre épuration et uniformisation : un danger bien réel

Le problème, si l'on en croit Heidegger, c'est qu'une telle présentation de la différence comme divergence par rapport à une essence pure et universelle procède d'une simplification arbitraire de la complexité naturelle de l'Être. Il était en effet bien plus simple de postuler l'existence d'un fonds commun à tous les étants qui est aussi l'Être le plus haut et le plus pur, et qui ne peut donc admettre en son sein l'idée même de différence, plutôt que d'essayer d'intégrer la différence entre les étants à la définition de l'Être. Pour Nancy, cette simplification ontologique est d'autant plus problématique qu'elle a eu de graves conséquences politiques. En présentant – à tort – l'unité absolue entre les hommes comme la vérité de l'humanité, la métaphysique a lancé tous les systèmes politiques de l'histoire occidentale à la poursuite d'un idéal qui éloigne l'humanité de ce qu'elle est vraiment, la menaçant alors de disparition. Preuve en est que plus les systèmes politiques de l'histoire occidentale se sont approchés de cet idéal d'immanence, plus ils se sont révélés dangereux. Un exemple marquant est l'aboutissement de la stratégie de libération recensée chez les peuples dits « primitifs » dans les fascismes de l'Europe du XXème siècle. Alors que l'idée d'exposer la différence afin de mieux s'en défaire posait déjà problème en termes d'éthique sous sa forme « primitive », puisqu'elle justifiait toutes sortes de conduites amorales lors de carnavals et rituels sacrificiels, celle-ci a pris une toute nouvelle ampleur en devenant sacrifice généralisé, un Holocauste. Dans le cas du nazisme, en effet, ce n'était plus seulement une victime sacrificielle qui était exposée et dont la suppression renforçait la cohésion sociale. C'est 17 millions de personnes jugées comme divergentes, 17 millions de juifs, d'homosexuels, d'handicapés, de tsiganes et d'opposants politiques, qui ont été désignés publiquement comme la différence faisant obstacle à la fusion au sein d'une communauté Aryenne « pure ». Cependant, comme le souligne Nancy,

> la logique de l'Allemagne nazie ne fut ... pas seulement celle de l'extermination ... du sous-homme extérieur à la communion du sang et du sol, mais aussi ... la logique

du sacrifice de tous ceux qui, dans la communauté 'aryenne', ne satisfaisaient pas aux critères de la pure immanence. (1990a: 36)

L'idéal nazi de l'Aryen étant lui-même une construction idéologique abstraite, il semble impossible pour des êtres faits de chair et d'os d'être à la hauteur de cet idéal. L'exigence de pureté et d'unité contamine inévitablement la communauté Aryenne, dont des membres seront toujours jugés pas assez blonds, trop petits, etc. Ainsi le sacrifice comme *holocauste* ne peut prendre fin que lorsqu'il ne reste plus personne à sacrifier.

Dans *La Déconstruction du christianisme*, Nancy remarque qu'une telle logique sacrificielle débridée est encore à l'œuvre aujourd'hui dans le terrorisme religieux. « Le "terrorisme" », écrit Nancy, « est la conjonction du désespoir et d'une volonté Uni-fiante » (2005a: 62). Les spécialistes de la question ne sauraient contredire Nancy sur ce point. L'idéologie extrémiste de Daech, par exemple, qui résulte d'un assemblage de doctrines salafistes et wahhabites, vise bien l'unité absolue d'une communauté fondée sur un islam soi-disant « véritable » par le sacrifice de toute personne qui n'en fait pas partie. Mais existe-t-il seulement un musulman suffisamment « pur » pour correspondre absolument à l'idéal salafo-wahhabite ? Et qui est en droit de juger d'une telle « pureté » ? On peut se le demander. Comme dans le nazisme, il semblerait donc qu'une telle logique immanentiste soit, au fond, suicidaire, ce qui explique pourquoi Daech s'attaque non seulement aux occidentaux athées, chrétiens ou juifs, mais aussi à d'autres musulmans, non-wahhabites, qui sont considérés comme hérétiques.

Par ailleurs, comme le souligne Nancy, les risques ne sont pas absents non plus de l'autre stratégie la plus courante de l'histoire politique occidentale, qui vise à atténuer les différences afin de faciliter la cohésion sociale. L'idéal d'égalité que cette stratégie politique promeut est, bien évidemment, souhaitable. Cependant l'histoire a prouvé que cet idéal, entre les mains des hommes politiques, a tendance à glisser vers l'uniformité. Les régimes totalitaires du XXème siècles et les Etats religieux intolérants de l'Europe médiévale en sont deux exemples parmi bien d'autres. Ce qui devait être une simple atténuation des différences individuelles en faveur de la cohésion sociale s'y est transformé en uniformisation par la force de communautés entières, dans lesquelles les seules opinions et convictions autorisées étaient celles du groupe.

Si ces exemples extrêmes nous apprennent une chose, selon Nancy, c'est que « les entreprises politiques … que domine une volonté d'immanence absolue ont pour vérité la vérité de la mort » (1990a: 35), que ce soit par une épuration sacrificielle sans fin ou une uniformisation détruisant tout ce qu'il y a d'humain en l'homme. De manière plus générale, Nancy voit dans ces cas extrêmes l'horizon de tout système politique fondé sur une recherche d'unité entre les hommes. Derrière chaque discours politique cultivant la peur d'une différence extérieure ou intérieure à la communauté se cache la menace d'une logique immanentiste dans laquelle peut se perdre toute l'humanité. L'unité, en fin de compte, semble donc être un idéal fondamentalement dangereux étant donné que, pour reprendre les termes de Tzvetan Todorov dans *La Conquête de l'Amérique*, il est malheureusement courant que « la différence se dégrade en inégalité; l'égalité, en identité » (1991: 186). Pour Nancy, il est donc clair que tant que l'histoire politique occidentale sera guidée par un idéal d'unité, « la communauté ne pourra qu'obéir … en simplifiant un peu, à peine, à un modèle soit fasciste, soit communiste » (1990a: 64).

La République française est-elle « une » ?

Pour qui a lu Nancy, il est alors désespérant de constater que l'Europe n'a pas appris de ses erreurs passées. Les expériences fascistes et communistes n'ont pas suffi à ternir l'idéal d'unité absolue que les occidentaux recherchent de plus belle aujourd'hui face au terrorisme. Le succès de la formulation *#JeSuis* en est la preuve. Or, à ce stade, on pourra opposer que le dépassement des différences et la fusion identitaire que propose l'affirmation « Je suis » sont à la fois momentanés et *strictement symboliques*. À première vue, la formulation *#JeSuis* n'engage pas la responsabilité des individus et ne peut avoir de conséquences politiques.

Mais est-ce vraiment le cas? On est en droit de se poser la question au vu d'événements récents. D'abord, le fait que le slogan « Je suis Charlie » a été récupéré par un collectif, « Le Printemps Républicain », créé en 2016 par Laurent Bouvet, qui a été critiqué pour ses prises de positions anticléricales. Ecrire « Je suis Charlie » s'apparente désormais à une manifestation de soutien à ce collectif, pour le moins controversé. Par ailleurs, comme le remarque Jean Baubérot, choisir de ne pas écrire *#JeSuisCharlie* sur les réseaux sociaux peut avoir de graves conséquences politiques. Fin 2017, la militante antiraciste Rokhaya Diallo a été évincée du Conseil National du Numérique pour avoir, entre autre, signé une pétition en 2011 intitulée « Pour la défense de la liberté d'expression, contre le soutien à *Charlie Hebdo* ». Ecrire, ou plutôt ne pas écrire « Je suis Charlie », n'est donc pas sans conséquences. Bien au contraire, nous ne sommes pas loin ici des dérives d'une stratégie politique visant l'unité absolue par uniformisation. Ce qui devait être une simple atténuation des différences individuelles en faveur de l'unité face au terrorisme semble glisser vers un système dans lequel les individus troquent leur singularité contre une identité globale, à laquelle ils doivent adhérer sans réserve. On comprend mieux la gêne ressentie par certains au moment d'écrire *#JeSuisCharlie* sur les réseaux sociaux, gêne qui tient donc plus de la formulation « Je suis » et de l'unité absolue qu'une telle tournure linguistique appelle de ses vœux, que du dernier des trois mots, Charlie, et sa ligne éditoriale provocatrice.

Or, pour Jean Baubérot, la formulation *#JeSuis* ne fait que mettre en lumière un glissement général de la laïcité française vers une approche toujours moins tolérante à l'égard des convictions individuelles, qui devient elle-même « une forme d'orthodoxie parareligieuse » (Sardier 2018; voir Sibertin-Blanc et Boqui-Queni 2015). Bien entendu, comme le rappelle le sociologue Jean-Paul Willaime, cette tendance n'est pas nouvelle. Avant même la rédaction de la loi de 1905, « le religieux était essentiellement perçu en termes de dangers, de risques » (2005: 76). Cette approche s'est perpétuée au cours des XXème et XXIème siècles au travers d'une vision de la laïcité dite « de combat ». Chère à Manuel Valls, Premier Ministre sous François Hollande, cette approche stricte de la laïcité assure que la montée de l'islam politique en France exige une attitude plus ferme envers l'islam et les religions en général.

Jugeant que la place des religions et leur visibilité dans l'espace public doivent être réduites au strict minimum, cette approche partage le regard ouvertement critique de *Charlie Hebdo* envers les religions et estime qu'il est inacceptable de ne pas soutenir unanimement le journal satirique, puisque cela serait justifier l'acte terroriste des frères Kouachi. La laïcité de combat s'oppose en cela à la vision dite « apaisée » prônant par l'intermédiaire du président de l'Observatoire de la Laïcité, Jean-Louis Bianco, un libre exercice des cultes sous réserve du respect de l'ordre public, tel que prévu par la loi de 1905. Une telle vision de la laïcité se voulant tolérante et inclusive à l'égard des communautés religieuses, elle s'est généralement montrée compréhensive envers les personnes critiquant la ligne éditoriale blasphématoire de *Charlie Hebdo*. Nicolas Cadène, rapporteur général de l'Observatoire de la Laïcité, est d'ailleurs souvent intervenu dans le débat public afin de rappeler que « Dire "je ne suis pas Charlie" ne veut pas nécessairement dire que l'on approuve les terroristes » (David 2015).

Depuis maintenant plusieurs années, la laïcité apaisée cède du terrain à la laïcité de combat, comme le prouve par exemple le vote du 24 janvier 2018, qui soumet les députés à la neutralité religieuse, le port de signes religieux ostensibles étant banni de l'hémicycle. C'est un nouveau tour de vis dans la laïcité de 1905 qui imposait la neutralité aux seuls agents de l'Etat. Le peuple étant libre de manifester ses convictions, ses représentants ne devraient-ils pas l'être aussi? Alors que progresse l'idée d'une uni(formi)té – sinon de fait, au moins comme idéal – de la République française, Jean Baubérot s'indigne: « La République est 'indivisible' sans être "une" pour autant: vous me le copierez cent fois! » (2018). Le philosophe Yvon Quiniou n'a en effet pas hésité à déclarer que, selon la Constitution, la « République est une, indivisible, laïque et sociale ». Une imposture intellectuelle, selon Baubérot, qui illustre parfaitement les dérives actuelles d'une République laïque à laquelle du même coup on « ajoute le "une" et enlève le "démocratique" » (2018). En effet, comme le rappelle Baubérot, l'article 1er de la Constitution décrit la République française comme « indivisible, laïque, démocratique et sociale », mais certainement pas « une ».

Nancy a donc raison: « l'Unité, l'Unicité et l'Universalité ... sont convoquées *de part et d'autre* dans l'affrontement mondial » (2005a: 61, je souligne). A l'exigence perverse de pureté de l'idéologie islamiste s'oppose la volonté occidentale – et particulièrement française – d'unité absolue, dont la formulation *#JeSuis* est le symbole. Une force unifiante s'oppose à une autre, et toutes deux menacent l'humanité, la première directement par la suppression violente de la différence, la seconde plus insidieusement, par uniformisation. Cependant, comme l'explique l'intellectuelle allemande Carolin Emcke dans un essai qui a fait grand bruit en Europe depuis sa parution en 2016: « Le dogme de la pureté et de la simplicité ne peut pas se combattre au travers d'une adaptation mimétique » (2016: 194). Afin de restaurer le principe de laïcité à sa version apaisée, mieux lutter contre l'idéologie islamiste, et plus généralement développer des politiques qui ne menacent pas l'humanité d'autodestruction ou d'uniformisation, « le plus urgent est de plaider pour l'impureté et la différenciation, parce que c'est ce qui contrarie le plus les haineux et les fanatiques dans leur fétichisme du pur et du simple » (Emcke 2016: 196).

#EgoCum: plaidoyer pour la diversité et le désœuvrement

Contre l'exigence de pureté islamiste donc, célébrons nos différences. Mais pour ce faire, il faut commencer par arrêter de voir dans l'immanence de l'homme à l'homme la vérité perdue de l'humanité. Il faut arrêter de considérer que la différence est fondamentalement négative, une forme de corruption d'un Être pur et universel. Ce combat doit alors se jouer sur le terrain de l'ontologie, et aboutir à une définition de l'Être qui intègre la différence en tant que telle. Encore une fois, selon Nancy, il faut alors se tourner vers Heidegger. Dans *L'Être et le Temps*, celui-ci propose de redéfinir l'Être de manière à donner un sens à la différence entre les étants grâce au concept de *Dasein*. Le *Dasein*, selon Heidegger, est l'être en tant que « là » de l'Être. Une telle proposition signifie que l'Être est toujours déjà être-dans-le-monde (*In-der-Welt-sein*). Chaque étant est l'Être tel qu'il est « là », dans le temps et l'espace. En cela, il est inévitablement singulier, unique, différent. En intégrant ainsi la différence à la définition de l'Être, on comprend alors immédiatement pourquoi l'idéal d'immanence absolu de l'homme à l'homme s'est révélé profondément dangereux au cours de l'histoire. Promouvoir l'unité absolue entre les hommes va en effet à l'encontre de la définition même de l'Être humain comme toujours déjà singulier, et ne peut donc se solder que par une aliénation de l'humanité. Célébrer les différences individuelles serait, au contraire, plus adéquat au regard de ce qu'est qu'Être humain.

Certains verront cependant dans cette célébration des différences la menace d'un individualisme radical menant à la dissolution des communautés humaines. Comment, en effet, sauvegarder la solidarité qui facilite la survie et l'épanouissement des hommes si la politique célèbre les différences plutôt que de travailler à l'unité ? C'est là que le concept de *Dasein* se révèle particulièrement intéressant. Dire que l'Être est toujours déjà être-dans-le-monde signifie en effet que la seule forme d'existence possible des étants est la coexistence. Être, c'est être-avec (*Mitsein*). Comme l'explique Nancy, « L'existence sociale de Descartes précède logiquement et chronologiquement la possibilité de l'énonciation d'ego sum – lequel, en s'énonçant, s'énonce d'ailleurs au moins à un autre [...] et si bien, peut-on dire, que *tout ego sum est un ego cum* » (2001: 117, je souligne). Accepter et célébrer les différences individuelles ne peut donc en aucun cas glisser vers un individualisme radical ni menacer sérieusement la vie en commun, puisque la solidarité – ou fraternité dira Nancy (1988: 97) – est partie intégrante de ce qui définit l'Être humain. Être, c'est à la fois être singulier *et* pluriel, individuel *et* social ; toujours déjà *ego cum*. Pour Nancy, Être signifie donc s'inscrire dans un réseau d'étants singuliers liés par une fraternité *inaliénable*. Comme l'écrit le philosophe :

> Nos existences, toutes, celles des humains et des autres vivants, celles des éléments qui leur font appui ou milieu, nourriture ou instrument. [...] Toutes ces existences [sont toujours déjà liées par rien d'autre que leur projection commune, qui fait monde, qui fait un monde et un monde de mondes différenciés. (2005b: 21–2)

C'est pourquoi, pour Nancy, il est urgent d'arrêter de voir dans la communauté un moyen de transformer l'humanité en ce qu'elle n'est pas (1990b: 101). Il s'agirait plutôt de comprendre enfin que l'humanité, de même que la communauté, « nous est donnée avec l'être et comme l'être, bien en deçà de tous nos projets, volontés et entreprises » (1990a: 87). C'est en ce sens que Nancy se fait l'avocat d'une communauté « désœuvrée », comme l'indique le titre de son fameux ouvrage de 1986.

La politique n'aurait en effet de sens que dans la valorisation d'un état de fait: la nature singulièrement plurielle et pluriellement singulière de l'Être humain.

Si on peut reprocher à Heidegger de ne pas avoir été jusqu'au bout de ses propres intuitions, réceptif qu'il était au mythe nazi d'une communauté Aryenne pure et parfaite, Nancy s'est au contraire montré particulièrement déterminé dans la promotion de cette nouvelle ontologie qui affirme que « l'être ne peut *être* qu'étant-les-uns-avec-les-autres, circulant dans l'*avec* et comme l'*avec* de cette co-existence singulièrement plurielle » (1996: 21). Et pour nous guider dans cette même voie, Nancy indique que « L'enjeu est désormais de ne plus penser [...] ni à partir de l'un, ni à partir de l'autre, ... mais de penser absolument et sans réserve à partir de l'avec » (1996: 54–5).

Il me semble que c'est bien cette priorité qui mobilise Plenel, Baubérot, et bien d'autres encore trop peu écoutés, contre les discours laïcistes de Manuel Valls. En proposant de masquer nos différences au profit d'une plus grande uni(formi)té entre les hommes, la laïcité de combat pense encore et toujours à partir de l'un, s'inscrivant ainsi dans une tradition ontothéologique de laquelle sont nées les expériences politiques les plus mortelles de l'histoire. C'est aussi cette priorité qui doit nous retenir au moment d'écrire *#JeSuis* sur les réseaux sociaux, l'opposition la plus efficace contre le fanatisme étant la célébration des différences plutôt que leur dépassement. Osons alors, avec Nancy, ne pas être Charlie et critiquer la ligne éditoriale de *Charlie Hebdo*, parce que c'est là la plus belle démonstration de liberté d'expression. Baubérot a raison de rappeler que celle-ci, de même que « le droit au blasphème, ne s'applique pas qu'au discours à l'égard des religions » (Sardier 2018). Osons être à la hauteur de la devise de la République française en célébrant une fraternité qui ne verse pas dans le désir d'immanence. Et sur Twitter marquons plutôt *#EgoCum*, « Je suis *avec* Charlie ». Une façon de dire que moi, française, marseillais ou bretonne, athée, musulmane ou juif, à la peau claire ou foncée, féru de poésie ou de séries américaines, qui aime une femme ou bien un homme, me joint à *chacun*, et qu'étant-les-uns-avec-les-autres, nous allons contrer le fanatisme non pas en dépit de nos différences, mais plutôt grâce à elles.

Bibliographie

AFP, « Philippe Lançon: parler de "guerre de civilisation" n'est "pas pertinent" », *lexpress.fr*, 29 juin 2015. <https://www.lexpress.fr/actualite/societe/philippe-lancon-parler-de- guerre-de-civilisation-n-est-pas-pertinent_1694326.html>.
Askolovitch, Claude, « Revue de presse particulière ... », *franceinter.fr*, 15 novembre 2017. <https://www.franceinter.fr/emissions/la-revue-de-presse/la-revue-de-presse-15-novembre- 2017>.
Baubérot, Jean, « "République est une et indivisible": la réponse de Jean Baubérot à Yvon Quiniou », *lemonde.fr*, 1er janvier 2018. <http://www.lemonde.fr/idees/article/2018/01/08/republique-est-une-et-indivisible-la-reponse-de-jean-bauberot-a-yvon- quiniou_5238621_3232.html>.
Biseau, Grégoire, Faure, Sonya, Bretton, Laure, Sardier, Thibaut, et Frantz Durupt, « "Je suis Charlie": de consensuel à conflictuel », *liberation.fr*, 5 janvier 2018. <http://www.liberation.fr/france/2018/01/05/je-suis-charlie-de-consensuel-a-conflictuel_1620694>.
David, Romain, « 30% des collégiens des quartiers populaires ne se sentent pas "Charlie" », *lefigaro.fr*, 23 septembre 2015. <http://www.lefigaro.fr/actualite-france/2015/09/23/01016-20150923ARTFIG00192-30-des-collegiens-des-quartiers-populaires-ne-se-sentent-pas-charlie.php>.
Emcke, Carolin, *Contre les racines: plaidoyer pour l'impur* (Paris: Seuil, 2016).
Heidegger, Martin, *Identität und Differenz* (Frankfurt am Main: Vittorio Klostermann, 2006).
——, *Was ist Metaphysik?* (Frankfurt am Main: Vittorio Klostermann, 1955).
Marlière, Philippe, « Emmanuel Todd and the Great *Charlie Hebdo* "Sham" », *Occasion*, Vol. 9, 2015, pp. 1–7.
Nancy, Jean-Luc, *La Communauté désœuvrée* (Paris: Christian Bourgois, 1990a).
——, *La Déclosion, Déconstruction du christianisme I* (Paris: Galilée, 2005).
——, *Etre singulier-pluriel* (Paris: Galilée, 1996).
——, *L'Expérience de la liberté* (Paris: Galilée, 1988).
——, « L'Insacrifiable », *Une Pensée finie* (Paris: Galilée, 1990b), pp. 65–106.
——, *La Pensée dérobée* (Paris: Galilée, 2001).
Riss, « Édito », *Charlie Hebdo*, n°1321, novembre 2017, p. 3.
Sardier, Thibaut, « Jean Baubérot: "Le droit au blasphème ne s'applique pas qu'au discours à l'égard des religions" », *liberation.fr*, 6 janvier 2018. <http://www.liberation.fr/france/2018/01/06/jean-bauberot-le-droit-au-blaspheme-ne-s-applique-pas-qu-au-discours-a-l-egard-des-religions_1620562>.

Sibertin-Blanc, Guillaume, et Boqui-Queni, Laëtitia, « La laïcité répressive. Anthropologie géopolitique de l'*homo laïcus* », *Multitudes*, 59(2), 2015, pp. 104–13.

Szafran, Maurice, « "Qui est Charlie": Emmanuel Todd, quand un intellectuel perd les pédales », *challenges.fr*, 4 mai 2015. <https://www.challenges.fr/politique/qui-est-charlie-emmanuel-todd-ou-quand-un-intellectuel-deraille_93462>.

Todd, Emmanuel, *Qui est Charlie?* (Paris: Seuil, 2015).

Todorov, Tzvetan, *La Conquête de l'Amérique* (Paris: Seuil, 1991).

Truc, Gérôme, *Sidérations. Une sociologie des attentats* (Paris: PUF, 2016).

Willaime, Jean-Paul, « 1905 et la pratique d'une laïcité de reconnaissance sociale des religions », *Archives de sciences sociales des religions*, 129, 2005, pp. 67–82.

BENOÎT LE BOUTEILLER

Un *nous* contemporain: réseaux sociaux, discours nouveau et addiction

En Octobre 2010, invité spéciale de la Techonomy conference au bord du Lake Tahoe, Eric Schmidt, alors président d'Alphabet, la maison mère de Google lâche cette phrase:

> il y a eu 5 exabytes d'information créée par la civilisation humaine depuis ces origines jusqu'en 2003. Aujourd'hui, cette même quantité d'information est créée en deux jours et le rythme s'accélère ... Les gens ne sont pas prêts pour la révolution technologique qui va advenir.[72]

Eric Schmidt ne précise pas les éléments qui lui permettent de soutenir cela. Cette proposition a fait l'objet de plusieurs études pour montrer son caractère approximatif.[73] Mais, malgré tout, le propos de Schmidt donne une idée du bouleversement vertigineux et rapide de la masse d'informations, des modalités de production et de diffusion de celle-ci. Une grande partie de la quantité d'information créée et échangée est le fait des réseaux sociaux, que ce soit les forums de discussion ou les messageries instantanées. Il n'est donc pas infondé d'émettre l'hypothèse que cette

---

[72] « There was 5 exabytes of information created between the dawn of civilization through 2003, but that much information is now created every 2 days, and the pace is increasing ... People aren't ready for the technology revolution that's going to happen to them. » Cité dans Martti Lehto, Pekka Neittaanmäki, *Cyber Security: Analytics, Technology and Automation*, Springer International Publishing Switzerland, 2015, p. 7.

[73] Parmi ces études citons celle menée par la School of Information Managment and System de l'Université de Californie à Berkeley. Il s'agit d'une étude dirigée par Kirsten Swearingen, intitulée *How much information 2003?* et consultable en ligne à l'adresse suivante: <http://www2.sims.berkeley.edu/research/projects/how-much-info-2003/execsum.htm>.

évolution si massive et subite a probablement bousculé en profondeur les modes de récits, les façons de construire celui-ci et de produire un sens individuel et collectif à partir de la narration. Or, le *nous* se bâti dans le terreau du récit commun, de la narration collective.

Jacques Lacan va construire une théorie à l'endroit des discours. Pour le psychanalyste français il existe différents types de discours qui sont en vérité des modalités spécifiques de lien social, de possibilités pour le sujet de s'inscrire dans le lien social, et ce, du fait de la structure du langage. À le suivre, nous pouvons avancer que le discours est le lien social, du fait d'articuler un *nous* au sujet. Une modification de modalité de discours induit donc une nouvelle modalité du *nous* et une nouvelle modalité subjective. Attachons-nous donc ici à regarder de quoi la narration contemporaine, fruit des réseaux sociaux, est faite et ce qu'elle indique du discours spécifique qui est en jeu. Ainsi, nous pourrons déduire les incidences sur le *nous*, dans sa dialectique à la subjectivité.

Pour cela, nous regarderons dans un premier temps comment cette narration contemporaine interroge la notion même de vérité. Puis nous verrons comment ce discours nouveau est impliqué dans une modalité inédite du mythe. Nous déduirons de ces articulations, à partir de l'exemple du Brésil, les incidences politiques de ce discours contemporain, fruit des réseaux sociaux. Enfin, nous proposerons de saisir la nature de la dépendance grandissante de nombreuses personnes à ces réseaux sociaux qui est loin de l'aliénation naturelle de l'humain à son prochain.

Vérité, semblant et post-vérité

Suivons ici l'évolution épinglée par Christian Salmon, éditorialiste de Médiapart, écrivain, essayiste et chercheur au Centre de recherches sur les arts et le langage du CNRS. Il est connu pour avoir détaillé et analysé en 2007 le *storytelling*, concept qu'il a lui-même particulièrement forgé et divulgué.[74]

---

74 Christian Salmon, *Storytelling. La machine à fabriquer les images et à formater les esprits* (Paris: La Découverte, 2007).

Un nous *contemporain: réseaux sociaux, discours nouveau et addiction*

Dans cette recherche, il met en évidence les mises en scènes de récits qu'il qualifie de dominants dans les sociétés contemporaines de l'époque. Ainsi les *storytelling* infusent les imaginaires et deviennent une technique de *management* de la communication des pouvoirs politiques et économiques. Il brosse le portrait des usages de ces *storytelling* dans les différentes sphères de la vie sociale et propose de démontrer comment cette construction narrative, « *machine à fabriquer des images* » dit-il, à « *formater les esprits* », n'est pas un phénomène venant du corps social, mais un instrument de domination, de manipulation du citoyen, du consommateur.[75]

Douze ans plus tard, 2019, le même auteur remet en question la pertinence cette notion de *storytelling* pour dire la narration contemporaine. Selon lui, nous sommes passé à une autre modalité de discours, une autre ère: celle du *clash*.[76] Ainsi, nous sommes passé à une narration se basant sur une volatilité des certitudes et la violence des positions. « *Shock and awe* », le choc et la stupeur: c'est une formule qui résume initialement une doctrine militaire issue des Universités de l'armée des États-Unis. Cette doctrine repose sur le fait que par la violence et la surprise, il est possible d'imposer une domination rapide sur son ennemi. Steve Bannon, l'ex-*spin doctor*, l'ex-conseiller en communication de Donald Trump a utilisé cette expression pour dire ce qu'est le nouveau mode de narration qui se construit et qui circule sur les réseaux sociaux.

Nous pourrions dire, bien sûr, que ce « *Shock and awe* » dans un *twitt*, au sein d'une conversation d'une groupe Facebook ou WhatsApp, c'est du semblant, que ce n'est pas le « *Shock and awe* » appliqué en 2003 lors de la guerre des États-Unis en Irak. Le semblant, cela signifie, en français, l'apparence, l'apparence trompeuse. Par extension cela indique l'insuffisance. Aussi, parlerons-nous d'un semblant de bonheur, d'un semblant de richesse.

Faire semblant, c'est faire l'acteur, c'est du *fake*. Ce mot anglais qui a pénétré largement dans l'usage des langues occidentales vient du latin *falx*, qui a donné *falsus*, qui signifie tromper. Semblant, lui aussi, mot d'origine latine, vient de *similare* qui veut dire paraître semblable, qui donnera *similis* qui signifie ressemblant, qui donnera *simulo*, qui peut être traduit en français

---

75   Ibid., p. 213.
76   Christian Salmon, *L'ère du clash* (Paris: Fayard, 2019).

par copier, imiter, feindre. L'événement, l'étymologie nous l'indique, *evenio*, en latin, c'est ce qui surgit. Or, un événement, c'est un fait de discours. C'est ce que nous enseigne les deux séminaires de Jacques Lacan qui se suivent, le 17 et le 18, « L'envers de la psychanalyse » et d'« Un discours qui ne serait pas du semblant ».[77] Nous pouvons à ce propos entendre ici la possibilité même de l'existence de la « fake news » : si l'événement est un fait de discours, il est possible de le construire, par le discours, ou au contraire de le nier par le discours aussi.

Dire de quelque chose que c'est du semblant, cela peut recouvrir une dimension péjorative. Or, et Lacan le rappel clairement dans le début de ce séminaire 18, le semblant, c'est ce qui a permis la naissance même de la science moderne. Il évoque cet exemple dès la première leçon du 13 janvier 1971 : c'est en effet en regardant le ciel que des savants ont pu déterminer qu'il y avait l'existence de constellation.[78] Le tonnerre aussi, c'est du semblant. C'est un semblant de la loi du divin nous dit-il.[79] C'est une croyance. Et nous pouvons dire que dans l'enseignement de Lacan, sa notion de semblant signe le retour de celle de croyance, précieuse dans la clinique.[80] À nous référer à cette première leçon du séminaire 18, nous pouvons faire ainsi un lien entre la fonction du tonnerre, avec son effet « *Shock and awe* » (en tant que semblant de la loi divine, en tant que semblant) et la fonction de l'hallucination (hallucination dont nous pouvons prendre acte dans la clinique et que nous pouvons repérer à l'endroit de cette construction d'événement, d'une nouvelle nature, que sont les « fake news »).

Qu'est-ce donc qu'un semblant, à partir de ce séminaire 18 ? Il nous est arrivé, vivant un temps dans l'Océan Indien, de voir surgir depuis les dessous de la peau de l'eau, une baleine. La baleine est. Avec ou sans notre regard. Qu'est-ce qui va nous toucher, jusque dans nos corps, à ce moment-là ? Ce qui va provoquer cela c'est précisément le bain de semblant dans lequel nous baignons, dans lequel nos êtres nagent. Le semblant, comme outil

---

[77] Jacques Lacan, Séminaire 17, *L'envers de la psychanalyse* (Paris : Seuil, 1991); Jacques Lacan, Séminaire 18, *D'Un discours qui ne serait pas du semblant* (Paris : Seuil, 2007).
[78] Jacques Lacan, Séminaire 18, *D'Un discours qui ne serait pas du semblant* (Paris : Seuil, 2007), p. 15.
[79] Ibid.
[80] L'importance de cette notion de croyance va rester chez Lacan jusque dans les dernières articulations de son enseignement.

conceptuel, est ici précieux pour comprendre pourquoi cet événement de la baleine est pour nous d'une autre nature, revêt un autre statut que la vue d'une voiture par exemple qui passerait sous notre regard. Le semblant, pour Lacan, à partir de ce séminaire, c'est une manière de dire comment l'imaginaire et le symbolique, en tant que registres, se nouent.

C'est un nouage de l'imaginaire et du symbolique qui convoque le sujet comme effet. Dès l'ouverture de ce séminaire de 1971 Lacan pose l'enjeu de ce concept de semblant, dans ce qui fait nœud entre l'image et le langage: c'est le moyen de saisir l'émergence subjective en rapport à la vérité. La notion de semblant implique donc un remaniement de la fonction de vérité. Dans le langage courant, ce qui est du semblant n'est pas vrai. Le semblant s'oppose donc à la vérité. Lacan va se fonder de sa notion renouvelée de semblant pour ré-articuler celle de vérité. Dans ce séminaire, Lacan va introduire aussi ceci: la notion d'agencement des semblants.[81] Ces agencements de semblants donc, entre eux, c'est, par le truchement de nœuds spécifiques entre l'image et le langage, un moyen efficace et précieux qui est à la disposition du sujet pour cerner le Réel.

C'est une production de sujet. Son invention en somme. C'est son discours. C'est cela le discours, en tant que catégorie, que Lacan crée au cours du séminaire précédent, le séminaire 17: un discours est un agencement singulier de semblants qui, en cernant le Réel, peut avoir un effet sur lui.

Nouveaux mythes?

Nietzsche le disait déjà, avec ses mots qui claquent:

> Qu'est-ce donc que la vérité? Une multitude mouvante de métaphores, de métonymies, d'anthropomorphismes, bref, une somme de relations humaines qui ont été poétiquement et rhétoriquement haussées, transposées, ornées, et qui, après un long usage, semblent à un peuple fermes, canoniales et contraignantes: les vérités sont des illusions dont on a oublié qu'elles le sont, des métaphores qui ont été usées et qui

---

81 Cette idée d'agencement nous fait, bien que Lacan ne les cite ici nullement, bien sûr largement penser au travail de Gilles Deleuze et de Félix Guattari sur cette question.

ont perdu leur force sensible, des pièces de monnaie qui ont perdu leur empreinte et qui entrent dès lors en considération, non plus comme pièces de monnaie, mais comme métal.[82]

Le discours revêt une forme de volatilité de la vérité. Alors, quoi de neuf finalement, hormis le mode de transmission – les réseaux sociaux – de ces vérités, ou « fake news »? En quoi cela signerait une nouvelle modalité de discours et donc une nouvelle modalité de lien sociale et donc une nouvelle modalité du *nous*? Lacan prononce une conférence en 1953 sous le titre suivant: *Le mythe individuel du névrosé, ou poésie et vérité dans la névrose.*[83] Dans cet exposé, le psychanalyste français démontre comment le cas de l'homme aux rats, exemple fameux de Freud, était l'effet singulier de l'histoire d'un collectif familial. La proposition lacanienne de « mythe individuel » fait référence au « *roman familial du névrosé* » de Freud. Allusion donc, mais la distinction est de taille: un mythe, contrairement à un roman, n'est écrit par personne. Collectif et individuel s'articulent: Claude Lévi-Strauss le soutien, par le prisme du mythe, le mythe étant pour lui un jeu combinatoire de signifiants. Lacan reprend cette proposition et soutient que « *le mythe est ce qui donne une formule discursive à quelque chose qui ne peut être transmis dans la définition de la vérité* ».[84] Et c'est par sa conception d'un inconscient qui émerge dans l'articulation des signifiants que Lacan fait dans son texte, comme il le fait avant et le fera après, référence à Claude Lévi-Strauss.[85]

> En 1958 Lévi-Strauss nous livre ce qu'il nommera la formule canonique du mythe: $Fx(a): Fy(b) \approx Fx(b): Fa\text{-}1(y)$, qui peut se lire de la façon suivante: la fonction X de a est à la fonction Y de b ce que la fonction X de b est à la fonction a-1 (ou 1/a) de Y. Le principe de cette formule est la triple dialectique possible: des termes entre eux (a et b), entre terme et fonction (y et b), et d'un terme sur lui-même (a et non-a, ou a-1).[86]

---

82 Friedrich Nietzsche, *Le livre du philosophe* (Paris: GF, 1991), p. 123.
83 Jacques Lacan, *Le mythe individuel du névrosé, ou poésie et vérité dans la névrose* (Paris: Le Seuil, 2007).
84 Ibid., p. 14.
85 C'est ce que nous montrons dans Benoît Le Bouteiller, « Lacan avec Saussure: des effets dans la clinique », dans *Ferdinand de Saussure, un siècle de structuralisme et de post-structuralisme*, sous la direction de Léon-Michel Ilunga (Paris: édition de l'Harmattan, 2018).
86 C. Lévi-Strauss, *Anthropologie structurale* (Paris: Plon, 1958).

Il s'agit donc d'un rapport spécifique de termes et de fonctions. Aussi, nous pouvons dire que le mythe est une modalité spécifique de rapport. Le rapport n'est pas la relation. Relation vient du latin *relatus* qui lui-même vient de *refero*. *Fero* signifie porter. Et le sufixe *re*, ici, a le sens de rendre. C'est ce sens que prend ce même suffixe dans le mot refroidir par exemple: rendre froid à nouveau. *Relatio* signifiait donc littéralement « porter à nouveau » et prendra ainsi le sens de récit. En effet, c'est le propre du récit que de *porter à nouveau* à la connaissance de l'auditeur, du lecteur la narration d'un fait, d'un événement, d'une pensée, qui ne sait pas dérouler ici et maintenant, à porter d'œil, d'oreille.

Le rapport a pour sens premier le revenu, le produit d'une chose. Il y a une dimension comptable. Le paysan pouvait dire par exemple que ce champ était d'un bon rapport. Ceci signifiait que le produit (économique) induit par l'exploitation de ce champ était important. Dans cet exemple, nous pourrions dire en somme: le champ entraîne, induit, implique la notion d'argent. C'est dans cette dimension de cause à effet que rapport prend donc ensuite le sens de désigner le rattachement d'une chose à une autre, le rattachement par lien logique, par lien de *logos*.

Le *logos*, dans l'art dit de rhétorique désigne la démonstration, la construction argumentative. Le *logos* est un des éléments du trépied de la rhétorique, les deux autre étant l'*ethos* et le *pathos*. L'ethos, c'est ce qui désigne le caractère, les habitudes, la manière d'être d'un individu. Et le pathos est traduisible par passion, souffrance, affect.

La relation tient à ces dimensions de l'*ethos* et du *pathos*. C'est de cela dont il est massivement question dans ces formes contemporaines de récits qui se produisent des réseaux sociaux. Le rapport, dans sa dimension de *logos*, en est exclu, forclos. Aussi, sans rapport, bien qu'il y ait des relations, ce discours n'est pas susceptible d'offrir les dialectiques structurelles essentielles pour se constituer en mythe.

Nous assistons à des communautés qui se créent, qui construisent et partagent une narration. Les psychologues démontrent depuis longtemps ce qu'ils appellent les biais cognitifs. Il s'agit des distorsions que l'individu inflige, sans s'en rendre compte la plupart du temps, à une information qui s'offre à lui, du fait d'un traitement cognitif particulier. Parmi ces biais cognitifs, il en est un particulièrement actif chez les humains. Il s'agit du biais dit de confirmation. Il s'agit de distorsions qui sont faites pour que le traitement de l'information s'inscrive dans ce que l'individu sait déjà, ce dont il est déjà persuadé, convaincu. C'est en somme une sélection qui va être opéré pour ne retenir de l'environnement que ce qui peut entrer dans les boîtes déjà constituées de la compréhension que l'individu a de cet environnement. L'individu va voir comme une évidence l'élément dont il peut se servir pour nourrir ce qu'il sait, ce qu'il croit déjà. Et avec la même efficacité, il va être aveugle à l'élément de ce même environnement qui pourrait l'amener à faire un pas de côté concernant ses certitudes.

Dans ces communautés qui se créent sur les réseaux sociaux, l'individu n'est même plus confronté à ce biais cognitif, très présent pourtant dans nos modalités humaines pour traiter l'information. Il n'est plus concerné par cela car ne rentre finalement dans son champ de perception que des déclinaisons de discours qui s'emboîtent dans la narration exclusive de cette dite communauté. Nous pouvons d'ailleurs nous interroger sur la pertinence de ce mot de communauté. Ce mot vient du latin *communis* lui-même composé de *cum*, qui signifie avec, ensemble et *munus*, qui signifie la dette. Aussi, communauté désigne un groupe qui a en partage une dette. De quelle dette s'agit-il? Faisons l'hypothèse qu'il s'agit de la dette de l'Histoire qui se véhicule par les histoires, les mythes. Or, nous l'avons montré, dans ce discours nouveau, il y a des relations mais pas de rapport. Il n'y a donc pas de mythe. C'est ceci sans doute que d'aucun nomme la post-vérité: une narration sans Histoire.

L'objet n'est donc pas de construire une dette commune envers la vérité de l'Histoire, de construire un *nous*, via le mythe, le *logos* du mythe, dans un jeu de rapport, mais de mettre en relation des « *Shock and awe* » sans le moindre souci pour quelconque histoire, quelconque vérité. Et nous repensons à la phrase de Hannah Arendt, pour qui « le sujet idéal du règne totalitaire n'est ni le nazi convaincu, ni le communiste convaincu, mais l'homme pour qui la distinction entre fait et fiction et la distinction entre vrai et faux n'existent plus ».[87]

---

87 Hannah Arendt, *Le système totalitaire* (Paris: Le Seuil, 1972), p. 224.

Des effets politiques

Ces réseaux sociaux ne sont pas, bien sûr, le fait des régimes totalitaires dont parlait Arendt. Mais avançons qu'ils sont le fait et le symptôme de formes totalitaires du discours capitaliste.

Le politologue britannique Jamie Bartlett dresse un diagnostic sans ambiguïté.[88] Selon lui la démocratie et les réseaux sociaux tels qu'ils existent aujourd'hui sont parfaitement incompatibles. Il est un signe frappant de ce capitalisme totalitaire au sein de la narration propre aux réseaux sociaux: l'économie des discours qui se construisent et circulent sur ces plateformes numériques fonctionnent sur un mode étonnamment similaire au *High-Frequency Trading*.[89] Et ceci est vrai sur trois plans au moins: il n'est pas possible pour un humain d'analyser, du fait du volume des informations et leur rapidité de production, le mécanisme en jeu; les évolutions de la bourse, du fait de ce *High-Frequency Trading*, tout comme les discours sur les réseaux sociaux, sont d'avantage influencés par les rumeurs que par les faits. Le cours d'une action ne reflète pas la performance d'une entreprise. La véracité prouvée d'un discours n'est pas sur les réseaux sociaux la garantie que celui-ci sera entendu. Cela n'est plus le critère premier; et, finalement, les propriétaires d'actions ne se soucient plus de ce qu'était le cours de telle action la vieille, tout comme tout un chacun ne regardera plus le propos avancé la veille, ni même un Président ne se souciera l'après-midi même du *twitt* du matin.

---

88 Jamie Bartlett, *The People Vs Tech: How the Internet Is Killing Democracy (and How We Save It)* (Kindle Edition, publié par Ebury Digital, 2018).

89 Le *high-frequency trading,* appelé en français Les transactions à haute fréquence, ou encore trading haute fréquence (THF ou *HFT*) sont l'exécution à très grande vitesse des transactions financières faites par des algorithmes informatiques. Ce *high-frequency trading* est une des catégories de ce qu'est appelé dans le monde de la bourse le *trading automatique,* c'est à dire les transactions financières basées sur la décision statistique. Gérant donc un volume considérable de données boursières en un temps extrêmement réduit, par une traitement *big data*, ce *trading automatique* est devenu parfaitement inaccessible aux analyses humaines, boursières traditionnelles.

Le soir de l'élection de Jair Bolsonaro au Brésil, le 28 Octobre 2018, plusieurs journalistes brésiliens et étrangers témoignent de cette scène troublante: des supporters du nouveau président élu crient leur joie en scandant « *Facebook! WhatsApp!* ».[90] Ils ne clament pas le nom du candidat vainqueur, mais de deux applications; ils ne crient pas l'avènement d'un homme, d'un parti, de projets politiques, mais des réseaux sociaux. Et c'était en effet probablement eux les vainqueurs de cette élection. Et ceci non pas tant du fait des manipulations importantes d'opinion véhiculées par ces réseaux sociaux durant la campagne. Mais bien plus profondément, parce que les GAFAM sont les nouveaux espaces où les systèmes de narrations se construisent et avec eux les nouveaux systèmes de vérités.[91]

Que s'est-il passé? La session du congrès brésilien a déjà commencé depuis quelques heures ce 17 Avril 2016. Un député prend la parole pour apporter sa voix en faveur de l'*empeachment* de la présidente Dilma Rousseff. Ce député dédit son vote « *à Dieu, à la famille, aux forces armées, contre le communisme et à la mémoire de Carlos Alberto Brilhante Ustra* », un des plus grands tortionnaires de l'époque de la dictature brésilienne, entre 1964 et 1985, dont a été victime, lorsqu'elle était jeune femme, Dilma Rousseff. Ces mots sont ceux de celui qui sera élu quelques temps après à la plus haute magistrature du pays. Après cela, il ne cessera de décliner ce type de discours de haine et sans argumentation à l'égard des femmes, des homosexuels, des indiens, des opposants politiques, des noirs. Il revendique son droit de tout dire, comme il l'entend.

Cet homme, Bolsonaro, depuis sa campagne électorale, est appelé par ses soutiens « le mythe ». Lacan le dit, « *tout mythe se rapporte à l'inexplicable du Réel* ».[92] C'est l'essence du mythe: dire là où il n'y a pas de mot, construire une narration à l'endroit du trou dans le tissu du langage. Ceci est une tentative des fascistes, des dictateurs depuis toujours. Quelle est donc la caractéristique de cette nouvelle promesse du tout dire dont

90 Images visibles par exemple à l'adresse suivante: <https://videos.bol.uol.com.br/video/apoiadores-de-bolsonaro-gritam-whatsapp-e-facebook-04024D1C3462E4A96326>.
91 GAFAM est l'acronyme d'entreprises du web: Google, Apple, Facebook, Amazon et Microsoft.
92 Jacques Lacan, Séminaire 8, *Le tranfert* (Paris: Seuil, 2001), p. 70.

Bolsonaro est un pathétique exemple ? Pour ce qui est du contenu du récit, tout d'abord remarquons une valorisation absolue du peuple, sans que nous ne sachions ce que recouvre ce mot.[93] C'est une valorisation du peuple au détriment des élites du système, sans que nous ne sachions non plus ce que recouvre cette expression.

C'est une valorisation du peuple au détriment de la démocratie. Dans la narration de ce mythe contemporain, le peuple doit protester violemment contre cet « autre » qui est responsable de la dépossession et ceux qui incarnent les élites du système sont des alliés de cet « autre ». Les solutions pour éliminer cet altérité de l'« autre », cette altérité qui vole la possibilité de jouir, les solutions sont simples, mais ne seront pas appliquées par ces élites. La démocratie, dans cette narration contemporaine, est l'organisation de société qu'il faut détruire pour permettre l'avènement de l'Homme, l'Homme fort qui s'est forgé seul, contre tous et qui ose tout dire. Ceci est un mécanisme assez classique dans les narrations fascistes. Ce qui est nouveau, c'est l'usage spécifique de la parole pour construire cette narration qui est la retranscription hors des réseaux sociaux d'un mode de parole qui leur est propre.

Bolsonaro dit tout haut le parler des réseaux sociaux. Dans ce mythe contemporain, l'Homme fort a un rapport spécifique à la parole: il écrase, en effet, chaque fois que c'est possible, le subtil, pour montrer comment il peut jouir, sans entrave, jouir sans entrave du seul fait de parler. L'obscénité du discours, l'injure sont valorisées, car c'est un signe de cette liberté, signe de cette liberté que nous pourrons enfin retrouver, cette liberté de jouir en parlant, sans entrave. Et cet Homme est le signe de l'*hypervirilité*, qui peut jouir, là aussi, sans restriction, libéré de l'effet féminisant du discours des élites du système. Dans ce mythe contemporain, l'Homme est l'incarnation de la Loi de la jouissance, au-dessus de toute autre loi. C'est cela que signifie le slogan de campagne de Jair Bolsonaro: « *Le Brésil au-dessus de tout, Dieu au-dessus de tous* ».[94] C'est un dieu obscure dont il est question, ce dieu obscure qu'évoque Lacan en fermant son séminaire en 1964 en parlant du

---

93 Mentionnons ici l'article brillant de Joseph Rouzel, *La langue de l'oppresseur*, où il évoque notamment comment la langue nazie « *martèle le signifiant* Volk *pour produire l'impression de servir le peuple* ». *Revue VST*, n. 141, p. 32.

94 « *Brasil acima de tudo, Deus acima de todos* ».

drame nazi.[95] C'est le dieu de la jouissance. C'est le dieu qui implique une haine qui doit se manifester, sans frein, comme un impératif, un impératif « au-dessus de tout et de tous », y compris au-dessus du savoir.

De fait, la haine ici est accolée à la passion de l'ignorance. Cet Homme puissant incarne en effet la déchéance du savoir. Le savoir est un objet d'exécration, un objet risquant justement de faire barrage à la jouissance. L'alliance de la haine et de l'ignorance, dans sa sauvagerie la plus brute, sont les garanties de l'efficacité du discours nouveau. Affranchi du savoir, du subtil, de la castration, nous pourrons … nous pourrons quoi ? Jouir, sans entrave. De Mussolini à Pinochet, ou pendant la dictature brésilienne, la transmission du mythe incarné par l'Homme fort était assurée par deux éléments qui s'unissaient: la société du spectacle qui était cultivée et l'avènement des mass-médias qui garantissaient la diffusion de cela. Le mythe fasciste traditionnel se servait de la société du spectacle au sens où « le spectacle est une vision du monde devenue effective, matériellement traduite. C'est une vision du monde qui s'est objectivé ».[96] Et donc pour diffuser ce spectacle, ils avaient besoin des mass-médias; ceux qui avaient pour caractéristique de s'adresser à tous, à partir de codes sociaux, culturels partagés. Ces deux éléments, la société du spectacle et les mass-médias ont été pulvérisé et ne sont plus que des souvenirs. Aujourd'hui, c'est les réseaux sociaux, eux même générateurs de ce discours nouveau qui va en assurer sa transmission.

Aliénation vs addiction

Le sujet humain a affaire à une forme d'aliénation naturelle à l'autre. Mais l'addiction que le nombre de personne ont aux réseaux sociaux n'est pas la marque de ceci. L'aliénation qui est le propre de notre humanité, Freud l'évoquait déjà. *Mais la dépendance grandissante aux réseaux sociaux n'est*

---

95   Jacques Lacan, Le séminaire 11, *Les quatre concepts fondamentaux de la psychanalyse* (Paris: Seuil, 1973), p. 246–7.
96   Guy Debord, *La société du spectacle* (Paris: Gallimard-Collection Folio, 1992), p. 17.

en rien à comprendre par le truchement de cette aliénation naturelle de l'humain à son prochain. Ces GAFAM, support de ces réseaux sociaux, ont la puissante caractéristique d'utiliser, d'exploiter nos particularités humaines, neurologiques, subjectives. Leur succès tient à cela. Ces emprises aux réseaux sociaux peuvent être similaires à tout type addictions. C'est un système qui se saisi du circuit dit de récompense et peut revêtir des fonctions structurelles pour un sujet de la même manière que la nicotine, le jeu en casino, même la cocaïne par certains aspects. Il relève bien ici d'une addiction, nous insistons, et non d'une aliénation naturelle que le sujet entretient à l'autre. Dès 1999, Kimberley Young décrit l'addiction à internet comme un terme regroupant potentiellement une large variété de comportements et de troubles du contrôle des impulsions dans l'utilisation d'internet.[97] Cet article de 1999 insiste déjà sur l'hypothèse d'un caractère particulièrement addictif des applications à visées sociales, relationnelles. Les recherches suivantes, nombreuses, ne feront que souligner ces premiers résultats.[98]

En 2009 un chercheur montre la spécificité de l'addiction à Facebook, hypothèses confirmées par plusieurs recherches postérieures.[99] La progression importante de ces dernières années en matières d'imagerie fonctionnelle a donnée de nouveaux éléments confirmant la puissance addictive de ces réseaux sociaux et la similitude de ces addictions avec d'autres formes plus classique de dépendances comportementales ou à des produits. Ces recherches montrent pour des sujets addicts aux réseaux sociaux des spécificités des zones cérébrales impliquées dans le circuit de récompense similaires dans d'autres addictions, avec des altérations du fonctionnement des circuits dopaminergiques. En 2012 une étude montre chez des sujets addicts à internet une diminution de la concentration des récepteurs à la

---

97 Kimberley Young, et al., « Cyber Disorders: the mental health concern for the new millennium », *Cyberpsychology & behavior*, 1999, pp. 475–9.
98 Citons à titre d'exemple celle de Alicia Douglas et al., « Internet addiction: Metasynthesis of qualitative research for the decade 1996–2006 », *Computers in Human Behavior*, 2008, pp. 3027–44.
99 Elisabeth Cohen, « Five clues that you are addicted to Facebook ». *CNN Health*, 2009, consultable à l'adresse suivante: <http://edition.cnn.com/2009/HEALTH/04/23/ep.facebook.addict/index.html>.

dopamine identique à celle retrouvée chez des sujets présentant une addiction à des drogues licites ou illicites.[100] Beaucoup plus récemment, Ofir Turel, professeur en systèmes d'information à l'université de Californie montre comment la spécificité de ces réseaux sociaux, notamment Facebook, opère neurologiquement pour nous en partie comme la cocaïne.[101] Nous rencontrons dans notre propre pratique des sujets en prise avec ces formes contemporaines d'addiction et qui présentent un tableau clinique identique à des sujets en situations d'addiction à des produits. Les réseaux sociaux prennent tout le temps, l'espace psychique du sujet, à qui il ne semble plus possible de gérer d'aucune manière la présence de cette consommation dans son existence.

Nomophobie est un mot récent. Il est la contraction de « *no mobile phobia* ». Il indique donc la phobie de certains individus à ne pas avoir leur téléphone portable avec eux. Ce mot a été élu mot de l'année 2018 par le *Cambridge Dictionary*. Je ne crois pas pour ma part que le terme de phobie soit adéquate pour nombre de ces individus. Il ne s'agit pas d'une phobie nouvelle qui serait apparue mais bien plus la manifestation symptomatique et douloureuse pour le sujet d'un état de manque ou d'une invasion d'angoisse à la perspective d'être dans cet état de manque, tout comme nous pouvons le voir sur le plan clinique dans toute autre addiction.[102]

---

100   H. Hou, et al., « Reduced striatal dopamine transporters in people with internet addiction disorder », *Journal of biomedicine & biotechnology*, 2012, p. 5.
101   Tout du moins pour le système impulsif du circuit de récompense, autant affecté pour les deux types d'addiction. Le système de frein est par contre plus conservé dans l'addiction aux réseaux sociaux que pour la cocaïne. Entretien à lire à l'adresse suivante: <https://usbeketrica.com/article/les-reseaux-sociaux-font-de-nous-des-pigeons-de-skinner>.
102   Il s'agit en effet dans les descriptions faites par les personnes elles-mêmes de formes classiques de *craving*. Ces nouvelles formes d'addiction sont à mettre en correspondance avec la mutation contemporaine du rapport d'objet et même plus fondamentalement avec la mutation de la nature même de cet objet, mutation si profonde qu'il doit, selon nous, être nommé autrement. C'est pour cela que nous avions proposé le concept de *novobjet*, dans Benoît Le Bouteiller, « O corpo na era da tecnociência: do objeto ao novobjeto », dans *Corpo e Cultura digital, dialogos interdisciplinares* (Belo Horizonte: Quixote+Do Editoras Associadas, 2018).

Un nous contemporain: réseaux sociaux, discours nouveau et addiction 115

Pour ouvrir

Nous avons affaire à un discours nouveau qui agrège des personnes sur des plates-formes, sans faire communauté, dont beaucoup entretiennent avec elles un rapport de dépendance, dans le réel du corps, comparable à toute autre addiction. Ce discours contemporain construit des histoires sans histoire, produit des passages à l'acte sans produire d'événements, tel que nous l'avons défini plus haut.

À la fin de l'année 2017, au début de l'année 2018, au Brésil, un *challenge* fait un succès considérable sur les réseaux sociaux. Il s'agit d'imiter une scène et de se faire filmer, à partir de toutes les déclinaisons possibles de ce même scénario: se faire tirer dessus, par un tireur invisible, imaginaire, et tomber, en faisant semblant d'être mort. Circulent sur les réseaux sociaux alors, de façon frénétique, ces petits films amateurs, tournés sur un parking, une salle de sport, à l'hôpital, un trottoir, dans une salle de bain, un restaurant, la plage, un supermarché … Des milliers de vidéos brésiliennes mimant le fait d'être touché par une balle et tombant, mort, au sol, sont partagées des milliers de fois. À l'origine de ce curieux phénomène, un clip, de Jojo Todynho, « *que tiro foi esse?* » Ce clip a été vu plus de 30 millions de fois sur les réseaux sociaux.

Quelques mois après, surgit un geste, qui va devenir une signature: le geste de Jair Bolsonaro qui mime le fait de tirer, avec ces doigts, et un large sourire. C'est ainsi qu'il ponctue ces phrases dans les réunions publiques: il mime qu'il tire dans la foule. Souvent, il ne dit même rien. Juste, il fait ce geste. Des gens tombant, frappé par une balle imaginaire, tiré par un assassin invisible; Et en face de cette mise en scène devenue une mode virale sur les réseaux sociaux, un homme, incarnation et produit d'un récit contemporain, tir sur une cible imaginaire.[103] Il fait de ce geste sa signature, signature qui sera reprise par des millions de brésiliens à leur tour sur les réseaux sociaux, signature d'un discours nouveau, signature de la grimace d'un *nous* qui prend nouvellement forme.

103 Le geste vise une cible invisible, mais les propos désignent les cibles bien clairement et l'augmentation des faits de violence au Brésil à l'égard des femmes, des homosexuels, des indiens, des noirs, des opposants politiques à Bolsonaro est explosive depuis le premier tour des élections présidentielles.

Bibliographie

Arendt, Hannah, *Le Système totalitaire* (Paris: Seuil, 2005).
Bartlett, Jamie, *The People Vs Tech: How the Internet Is Killing Democracy* (Ebury Press, 2018).
Débord, Guy, *La Société Du Spectacle* (Paris: Gallimard, 1992).
Douglas, Alecia C., et al., « Internet Addiction: Meta-Synthesis of Qualitative Research for the Decade 1996–2006 », *Computers in Human Behavior*, vol. 24, no. 6, September 2008, pp. 3027–44.
« Five Clues That You Are Addicted to Facebook », *CNN*, <http://edition.cnn.com/2009/HEALTH/04/23/ep.facebook.addict/index.html>, vu le 1ᵉʳ janvier 2019.
Hou, Haifeng, et al., « Reduced Striatal Dopamine Transporters in People with Internet Addiction Disorder », *BioMed Research International*, 2012.
Lacan, Jacques, and Jacques-Alain Miller, *Le Mythe individuel du névrosé* (Paris: Seuil, 2007).
——. *Les Quatre concepts fondamentaux de la psychanalyse* (Paris: Seuil, 2014).
——. *Le Séminaire, livre VIII : le transfert* (Paris: Seuil, 2001).
——. *Le Séminaire. Livre XVIII D'un discours qui ne serait pas du semblant* (Paris: Seuil, 2007).
le Bouteiller, Benoît. « Lacan Avec Saussure: Deseffets Dans Laclinique », *Ferdinand de Saussure: Un Siècle de Structuralisme et de Post-Structuralisme*, no. 1, 2018, p. 357.
Lehto, Martti, « Phenomena in the Cyber World », *Cyber Security: Analytics, Technology and Automation*, eds Martti Lehto and Pekka Neittaanmäki, Springer International Publishing, 2015, pp. 3–29.
Lévi-Strauss, Claude, *Anthropologie structurale* (Paris: Plon, 1958).
Nietzsche, Friedrich, *Le Livre du philosophe* (Paris: Flammarion, 2014).
Rouzel, Joseph, « La langue de l'oppresseur », *VST – Vie sociale et traitements*, vol. N° 141, no. 1, février 2019, pp. 28–33.
Salmon, Christian, *L'Ere du clash* (Paris: Fayard, 2019).
——, *Storytelling: La Machine à Fabriquer Les Images et à Formater Les Esprits* (Paris: La Découverte, 2007).
Young, K., et al., « Cyber Disorders: The Mental Health Concern for the New Millennium », *Cyberpsychology & Behavior: The Impact of the Internet, Multimedia and Virtual Reality on Behavior and Society*, vol. 2, no. 5, 1999, pp. 475–9.

MARIANNE GODARD

La communauté comme passage: l'éthique du poème d'Henri Meschonnic

La théorie littéraire, en ouvrant un questionnement sur nos épistémologies et sur la manière dont les œuvres construisent nos représentations, peut avoir un caractère utopique. La pensée de Meschonnic s'inscrirait dans cette vision, dans une œuvre autant théorique que poétique, écritures qui sont pour lui interreliées et concrescentes. Ainsi, on retrouve dans le recueil de poésie *Nous le passage* (1990), la création d'un texte/espace où se fabrique une utopie du commun, où un singulier anonyme se pense comme peuple par l'expérience de la voix et du corps.

Le sujet du recueil est sans frontières: il n'est pas « individu », soit atome insécable et séparé, mais sujet ouvert au monde, incliné vers l'autre. Nous aborderons dans cette discussion comment le sujet singulier se pense comme « nous », par une dissolution de ses frontières et une remise en question du processus même de nomination. Puis il s'agira de voir comment ce sujet se définit comme potentialité-devenir, ouvert à une altérité qui lui est consubstantielle. Finalement, nous verrons comment s'insère le lecteur dans cette vision utopique, par la performativité même du poème. Parce qu'on écrit toujours à, parce que le tracé d'une singularité est politique, il s'agira de réfléchir à la littérature comme expérience du commun: comment un livre crée un lieu distinct où le *je* peut exister devant et avec un *tu*.

Pour Meschonnic, le poème est « cet état naissant des modes de signifier, cette invention de l'historicité radicale des manières de dire, de sentir, de s'entendre soi et les autres ».[104] La poésie n'est donc pas quelque chose qui doit se concevoir comme étant séparé du « langage ordinaire ». Elle

---

104 Henri Meschonnic, *Politique du rythme, politique du sujet* (Lagrasse: Verdier, 1995), p. 17. (L'abréviation PRPS sera dorénavant utilisée pour citer cet ouvrage.)

n'invente pas un autre monde, mais « transforme le rapport qu'on a avec celui-ci ».[105] Si la poétique a pour interrogation première l'étude de la valeur des œuvres, de distinguer la chose littéraire de ce qui n'en est pas, elle pose également la question des valeurs: valeurs non pas au sens des normes existantes, mais au sens où l'œuvre est capable, à partir de son travail de création, de créer un nouvel espace de partage, de nouvelles conditions pour fonder un espace d'interrelation entre les sujets. Selon Meschonnic, la poétique ne se conçoit pas comme étant séparée de l'éthique, car « c'est par le langage qu'un sujet advient comme sujet »:[106] à l'encontre des modèles traditionnels qui considéraient le sujet comme préexistant au langage, il s'agit, à la suite de Benveniste, de penser le langage comme la condition de l'individuation.

Le sujet est ce qui se constitue dans l'acte même d'énoncer et il ne se confond donc pas avec le sentiment d'« être soi-même » ou une permanence de la conscience. Se réalisant à mesure qu'il s'énonce, il est « la personne, l'acteur, la fable qu'il est lui-même pour lui-même »,[107] tension qui fait en sorte qu'il est un travail constant, et toujours inscrit dans un rapport:

> la conscience de soi n'est possible que si elle s'éprouve par contraste. Je n'emploie *je* qu'en m'adressant à quelqu'un, qui sera dans mon allocution un *tu*. [...] Le langage n'est possible que parce que chaque locuteur se pose comme *sujet*, en renvoyant à lui-même comme *je* dans son discours. De ce fait, *je* pose une autre personne, celle qui, tout extérieure qu'elle est à « moi », devient mon écho auquel je dis *tu* et qui me dit *tu*.[108]

Aucun des deux termes ne se conçoit donc sans l'autre, et cela particulièrement pour le sujet du poème, qui porterait à son maximum ce principe d'altérité reconnu par Benveniste dans le champ du langage. Tel que théorisé par Meschonnic, le sujet poétique n'est toutefois pas à confondre avec l'auteur empirique ou éditorial, il n'est pas non plus un

---

105 Henri Meschonnic, *La rime et la vie* (Lagrasse: Verdier, 1990), p. 108.
106 PRPS, 376.
107 PRPS, 202.
108 Émile Benveniste, *Problèmes de linguistique générale*, t. 1 (Paris: Gallimard, 1966), p. 260.

individu qui exprimerait une intériorité préexistante au discours. Ce concept, se rapprochant peut-être un peu plus de la notion d'*ethos*, renvoie à une réalité qui n'existe que par et à travers le texte: le sujet n'existe pas avant le poème, il se fait dans l'écriture et la lecture.

Sa dimension éthique est alors centrale, car il devient, par la lecture, un agent de trans-subjectivité: « l'activité du poème fait du texte tout entier un *je*, et transforme par là le *je* du lecteur, en sorte qu'il participe, même, encore une fois, s'il ne le sait pas, de ce *je* nouveau, continu, contagieux, historique et trans-subjectif ».[109] En gardant à l'esprit que la littérature peut être productrice d'un savoir être, nous verrons dans le recueil *Nous le passage* comment le poème chez Meschonnic est le lieu d'une critique de la dualité individu-société, qui met à l'horizon une question éthique, celle du nous.

Le sujet de *Nous le passage* est un sujet nomade, à l'identité instable: il ne possède pas d'attaches à un lieu précis et ses propres frontières identitaires et corporelles sont constamment remises en question. D'un poème à l'autre il ne cessera d'être en mouvement, car demeure en lui un besoin fondamental de mobilité:

> je marche une ville dans la ville
> comme l'absence
> avec
> les yeux qu'elle a pour la vie
> pas de hâte pas de lenteur
> je longe des maisons vides
> elles donnent sur des rêves de rues on y serre des mains de pierre
> les visages portent des ruines
> fuir
> avant les murs[110]

Le monde qu'il traverse est lui-même caractérisé par une certaine instabilité. Ici, cette ville explorée se dédouble et s'emboîte, entre une ville aujourd'hui absente, qui pourtant continue à exister par le regard du sujet, et celle dont il « longe [l]es maisons vides ». Même dire qu'elle est

---

109   PRPS, 192.
110   Henri Meschonnic, *Nous le passage* (Lagrasse: Verdier, 1990), p. 10. (L'abréviation NP sera dorénavant utilisée pour citer cet ouvrage.)

« explorée » suggère une permanence qu'elle n'a pas: le sujet ne marche pas « dans la ville » ou « à travers » cette dernière, il « marche une ville », et elle semble alors se construire et se dérouler dans son mouvement même, se créer par la marche.

De façon similaire, le sujet du poème doit pouvoir bouger afin d'exister. À la fin du poème se dessine une violence latente, comme un impératif: « fuir/avant les murs ». Cette phrase infinitive constitue un point d'arrêt autant par la disposition graphique du verbe que par sa concision qui contraste avec les autres phrases plus longues du poème, ce qui contribue à lui conférer sa gravité. Fuir, « avant les murs », donc avant l'emprisonnement et l'immobilité, qui s'oppose au « je marche » ouvrant le poème. Cette menace est rendue sensible par les observations du sujet, des « rêves de rues » où l'on « serre des mains de pierre », où « les visages portent des ruines ». Est décrite une immobilité qui s'inscrit dans la chair même, le corps se pétrifiant: le visage, élément intime et porteur d'identité, porte ici la trace d'une destruction qui lui confère des caractéristiques non organiques, figées, et les « mains de pierre » semblent pouvoir se resserrer sur celles qu'elles tiennent.

Après ce poème, le 2e du recueil, cette marche continuera: pas nécessairement comme fuite d'une chose dont le sujet s'éloignerait, mais comme nécessité. Demeure toutefois dans certains poèmes une précarité sous-jacente:

> nous changeons de couleur
> selon le sol où nous marchons
> pas pour nous cacher
> puisque la peur nous reconnaît[111]

Si une menace semble toujours planer, puisqu'est écartée l'intention potentielle de se cacher, cette peur personnifiée pouvant identifier le sujet n'est pas un élément antagoniste. Elle accompagne plutôt son mouvement, et peu à peu, sera apprivoisée: « nous avons encore peur de la peur /, mais la peur nous mange dans la main / et nous endort quand elle veille ».[112]

---

[111] NP, 20.
[112] NP, 46.

Et si le corps du sujet pouvait être marqué par l'immobilisme, de façon analogue son déplacement le modifie corporellement. Entre son corps et le monde qu'il traverse, une relation de perméabilité s'instaure: ici, c'est « nous » qui « changeons de couleur / selon le sol où nous marchons », ailleurs, ce sont « les rues comme nous [qui] sont devenues bleues ». En effet, le sujet semble presque partager sa peau avec le monde qui l'entoure:

> la lumière amoureuse
> et nous le ciel sur la peau
> jusqu'à
> jamais et un jour[113]

Cette personnification de la lumière lui confère un caractère physique qui s'incarne immédiatement avec l'adjectif « amoureuse »: l'image qui est créée est celle d'une lumière qui chercherait véritablement à caresser, à toucher. Matérialité qui est reprise par la deuxième ligne, où ce n'est pas la lumière ou le soleil qui est « sur la peau », mais le ciel même, élément beaucoup plus intangible, mais qui pourtant recouvre le corps du sujet. Puis, d'une perméabilité, il passe à une dissolution complète de ses frontières corporelles:

> la lumière était un trou était un cercle de cercles
> dont nous-mêmes nous irradions
> et nous nous diluons comme elle
> dans un vent qui s'accroche à un arbre
> devant un pont[114]

Si le « nous » émane de la lumière, élément déjà incorporel, il le fait en irradiant, en se répandant dans toutes les directions. Ce mouvement n'est toutefois pas une expérience céleste, il est ramené à quelque chose de tangible, d'accessible. Le sujet se dilue *dans* quelque chose, « un vent qui s'accroche à un arbre ». Cela permet d'appréhender l'expérience, autant par la matérialité des éléments (on peut imaginer un vent

---

113 NP, 12.
114 NP, 16.

« s'accrocher » à un arbre), que par la précision donnée du lieu, « devant un pont », complément circonstanciel mis en valeur par sa séparation d'avec le reste de la phrase, autonomie inhabituelle qui lui confère alors plus d'importance.

Le corps comme entité physique sensorielle n'est donc plus quelque chose d'uni, il est mouvant, fluide, et l'identité du sujet se veut continue plutôt que discontinue, au sens d'individu, d'unité indivisible qui est séparée du monde. Et cette continuité se traduit également par la possibilité de partage: si le sujet se dilue dans la lumière, il le fait « devant un pont », lieu concret et terrestre; le ciel, élément rattaché traditionnellement au divin, réside sur sa peau; et la locution adverbiale « à jamais » qui appelle l'infini, est ramené à taille humaine de façon paradoxale, puisque « jusqu'à » implique un point dans le temps, un événement (alors qu' « à jamais » se soustrait au temps), et que « et un jour » donne un caractère humain à cette temporalité inaccessible, la transforme en un infini à notre portée.

L'omniprésence de la minuscule dans le recueil et l'absence de signe de ponctuation participe également de cette idée de continuité.[115] Les repères traditionnels permettant de savoir comment arrêter ou continuer les phrases sont absents. L'avant et l'après sont ouverts, et les énoncés ne sont plus divisés ou hiérarchisés. En effet, si la poétique de Meschonnic vient remettre en question le caractère dichotomique de l'identité et de l'altérité, et penser différemment ce rapport, elle le fait conjointement à une critique du langage vue comme étant fait d'unités discontinues et hiérarchisées, et du sens comme résidant dans les mots, plutôt que dans tout le discours.

Cette recherche de continuité se traduit donc également par un rapport particulier à la nomination:

> ce qui ressemble à la nuit nous connaît par notre nom
> car même après le sommeil nous sommes tout de nuit
> une matière d'avant nous et après nous
> elle se rassemble ou se disperse
> ce sont ses mouvements
> que nous suivons elle est hors de nous

---

[115] Sauf à la p. 50, où le poème est précédé d'une séquence narrative où l'on trouve majuscules et ponctuation.

> ou en nous une voix qui marche ou un rêve qu'on chasse des mains
> les noms les noms ne font pas partie de nous
> leurs lettres se terminent en flammes qui prennent sur nous
> de cette brûlure nous naissons[116]

Dans ce poème, le sujet *n'est* pas cette nuit, mais plutôt fait « de nuit », composé de cette « matière », instable autant dans sa temporalité (elle est « une matière d'avant nous et d'après nous ») que dans sa spatialité (« elle se rassemble et se disperse », « elle est en nous ou hors de nous ») et définissant encore une fois le sujet comme mobile. Au centre du poème, « ce sont ses mouvements » crée paradoxalement un moment de suspension dans la lecture qui en intensifie le contenu; cette ligne est la plus courte du poème, ce qui contribue peut-être à cet effet de concentration, mais c'est surtout la division entre « mouvements » et sa relative « que nous suivons » qui, après coup, crée un effet d'interruption, ces deux éléments syntaxiques étant traditionnellement disposés en continu. Puis, la continuité graphique de la relative « que nous suivons » à une nouvelle phrase participe également à la production du sens, l'action de suivre étant traduite par la dynamique de lecture de la ligne même et l'absence de ponctuation ou de séparation graphique.

Ce besoin de mouvement au centre du poème s'incarne alors à même le langage. Le sujet du poème refuse la nomination: « les noms les noms ne font pas partie de nous ». La répétition de « les noms », incarne la pluralité du GN et renforce son caractère impersonnel, qui vient s'opposer à « notre nom » en début de poème. Ce refus traduit la critique d'une vision du sens comme résidant dans le mot, et la sacralisation subséquente du mot et des noms, qui fait oublier et efface le sujet du discours comme élément producteur du sens. La violence de cet effacement potentiel, s'incarne ici par le feu: les noms ne font pas partie du « nous », mais ils le brûle, adhère à sa peau (les « flammes qui prennent sur nous »). Le « nous » est le combustible même de ce feu, qui devient alors sa naissance, renvoyant à cette idée que le sujet est une lutte toujours recommencée, où chaque combat est alors un « baptême du feu ».

---

[116] NP, 15.

« Notre nom » serait en fait anonyme: « les noms tous les noms ensemble / font une absence de nom / plus ils se poussent plus ils serrent / l'anonymat / qui fera de notre nom une phrase ».[117] On pourrait deviner dans ce poème l'horreur d'un nombre de morts tellement grand qu'il fait de « tous les noms ensemble » une « absence de nom ».[118] Mais un renversement est opéré: l'anonymat n'est plus synonyme de souffrance ou de perte, il n'est plus une absence de nom. Une autre expérience de l'anonymat émerge peut-être, qui permettrait au vide de se transformer en un espace ouvert à la potentialité, pour que le « notre nom » puisse émerger, non pas comme *un* nom ou individu, mais comme phrase, continue. Le commun qui réside de façon inhérente dans le « nous » serait cet anonymat partagé, qui ne serait pas à comprendre comme un manque, mais plutôt comme, de par ce partage, la potentialité d'un plein.

Le nous serait donc un espace qui se doit d'être vide afin d'être rempli par l'indétermination et la possibilité de mouvement, ce qui définit un passage. Et il abrite un lieu où peut être la différence:

> à l'intérieur des lettres
> d'autres lettres
> à l'intérieur du corps
> nos autres corps
> comme une langue
> à chaque moment différente
> que nous sommes toujours au commencement d'apprendre[119]

Dans ce poème, le corps comme chaque lettre semble être une forme de palimpseste, une œuvre qui laisse supposer et apparaître des traces de versions antérieures. En effet, quelque chose « d'autre » est à l'intérieur du sujet énonçant, comme une génétique de la parole, mais qui ne serait pas linéaire (définie par un axe passé-présent-futur) comme le manuscrit du palimpseste: cette « langue » est à chaque moment en train d'être apprise. Il y a une redécouverte incessante, non pas dans une dynamique de l'inconnu vers le connu, ou du défrichage, quiréduirait cette altérité. C'est

---

[117] NP, 29.
[118] Faisant écho aux poèmes aux pages 34, 50 et 77.
[119] NP, 33.

plutôt un renouvèlement de l'inconnu au centre du sujet qui a lieu: « je connaissais des réponses /, mais les questions me connaissent / mieux car jour nuit elles / m'inventent ».[120] Au centre d'un corps et d'une identité mouvante, réside un espace, une ouverture presque aliénante:

> et ce bleu est tellement nous que quelque chose fond en nous
> et se dissout dans le ciel quand nous regardons
> le changement qui se fait
> loin
> dont nous sommes plus près que
> de ce loin qui est en nous[121]

Le sujet du poème va d'un mouvement de concentration (« et ce bleu est tellement nous que quelque chose fond en nous ») à un mouvement de dispersion (« et se dissout dans le ciel quand nous regardons ») avant d'être pris entre les deux, ou plutôt d'être les deux en même temps: « le changement qui se fait / loin / dont nous sommes plus près que / de ce loin qui est en nous ». Quelque part, ailleurs, un changement a lieu auquel le sujet s'identifie: il en est près, intérieurement ou physiquement – et en même temps il est loin de cet autre ailleurs (nommé simplement « ce loin ») qui se situe en lui. Ce qui est « en nous » est pourtant doublement éloigné, presque inaccessible dans son étrangeté, un loin qu'on ne peut pas approcher. Cette tension entre dispersion et concentration est ouverture à l'altérité, que celle-ci soit représentée par le réel physique où le sujet n'est plus enraciné en lui-même, délimité et indivisible, ou par cette altérité irréductible résidant en son centre.

Ce qui semble demeurer au centre du sujet énonçant c'est cette potentialité, espace qui pourrait être passage. Mais ce dernier n'est pas stable ou intemporel:

> les rues comme nous sont devenues bleues
> les passants presque invisibles
> sont des traces de mouvements et
> nuit sur nuit on voit dedans[122]

---

120   NP, 61.
121   NP, 18.
122   NP, 30.

Ici, le passant, entité déjà éphémère, est encore plus désubstantialisé puisqu'il est « presque invisible ». Il ne laisse pas des traces de son mouvement, il est ces traces mêmes. Ces dernières à l'inverse matérialisent le mouvement et lui donne une densité temporelle. Le sujet nomade du poème n'est toujours pas dans une dynamique de la découverte – il passe par où d'autres sont passés. La répétition/superposition « nuit sur nuit » crée également une densité, et ce qui semble être un espace: on voit « dedans » cette « nuit », ou surtout « dedans » ces « traces de mouvements ». Cela implique alors que le fait même de passer crée un lieu avec un « dedans », un passage, ce que soutient l'écho de « mouvem*ents* » à « ded*ans* ». Ce dedans n'est toutefois pas une reprise du mythe de l'intériorité: il n'est pas porté par le « je », mais par un « nous », une intériorité plurielle.

Le passage, défini comme l'action de passer, mais aussi l'endroit où l'on passe, est dans ce recueil l'un et l'autre et ne peut se réaliser que grâce à l'autre, c'est-à-dire qu'il se créerait comme espace par le mouvement même. Ce double sens est présent dès le titre du recueil, où le « nous » peut autant incarner ce lieu que le mouvement: nous, lieu du passage et nous qui faisons l'action de passer. Cela traduit alors cette perméabilité du sujet avec le monde, et du monde avec lui. Et de façon réciproque, c'est cette action de passer et d'être de passage qui créerait un espace où peut exister le « nous ». Ainsi, au contraire d'une formulation telle que « nous sommes le passage », où le premier terme de l'identification serait évidé au profit du second, « nous le passage » tend vers une relation de circularité et de co-dépendance entre les deux termes. « Nous » qui dès la première lettre du titre, commence par un rappel potentiel du feu nécessaire à la naissance d'un commun qui ne serait pas synonyme d'identité et de fixité, mais d'anonymité et de mouvement.

Si le sujet du recueil est caractérisé par ce « passage », le poème l'est de façon intrinsèque également. En effet, le lecteur du poème est partie prenante de la situation d'énonciation, sa place étant réservée en creux ou en négatif dans le poème, puisqu'il peut partager ou reprendre à son compte la posture énonciative du locuteur, moduler le contenu de l'énoncé pour soi-même. Cet espace, ce passage existe au sein du poème, qui peut être reénoncé indéfiniment. Il se rend perméable et malléable à toute nouvelle énonciation et dans ses blancs, le texte poétique peut procéder dans tous les sens: cela constitue une relance inscrite au cœur même du poème, une possibilité de redéploiement dans chaque performance individuelle, dans chaque lecture. Le lecteur comme autre est donc invité à emprunter ce passage ouvert par le sujet du poème.

Bibliographie

Benveniste, Émile, *Problèmes de linguistique générale*, t. 1 (Paris: Gallimard, 1966).
Meschonnic, Henri, *Nous le passage* (Lagrasse: Verdier, 1990) (NP).
——, *Politique du rythme, politique du sujet* (Lagrasse: Verdier, 1995) (PRPS).
——, *La rime et la vie* (Lagrasse: Verdier, 1988) (RV).

ANDREA PERUNOVIC

#NousSommes: refondation onto-axiologique de la confiance

Chaque césure brutale dans la continuité de la vie quotidienne d'une communauté, chaque événement traumatique et/ou tragique, qui vient rompre le cours ordinaire des choses, entraîne une crise généralisée de la *confiance*. Ces brusques *réveils* provoquent souvent les réactions collectives de sujets sociaux, auparavant « paisibles », « sereins »; des sujets en fait *serviles* au sein de relations de pouvoir *encore* non contestées. Des sujets aliénés et divisés, pris de torpeur, d'un désir irrésistible de dormir, et comme le suggère Guy Debord, avec le « spectacle » faisant office de « gardien de ce sommeil ».[123]

Le phénomène #NousSommes auquel nous allons nous intéresser ici, cette construction linguistico-numérique, mais aussi ontologique, politique ou encore éthique, semble représenter un nouveau paradigme des réactions collectives, qui n'appelle au fond, à rien d'autre qu'à une refondation de la confiance bousculée. Refondation comme une prolongation du mauvais rêve. Mais en quoi consiste généralement cette « prolongation du mauvais rêve » qui constitue la refondation de la confiance? Derrière la métaphore du « rêve » empruntée à Debord, et derrière notre propre métaphore du « réveil » (comprise ici dans un sens restreint, quasiment ironique), se décèlent des phénomènes sociaux bien particuliers, des phénomènes se répétant dans presque chaque situation d'« après-choc », choc survenu dans une société qu'il affecte dans son ensemble. Se manifeste alors une manipulation fiduciaire[124] à l'œuvre, destinée à amortir le choc, garantir

---

123   Guy Débord, *La Société du spectacle* (Paris: Gallimard, 1996).
124   Le terme « fiduciaire » doit être compris ici non dans son sens le plus commun, relevant du domaine purement financier, mais dans celui, plus large, qui fait référence à tout phénomène relevant de la confiance.

la subsistance d'une continuité menacée par des événements s'imposant comme des ruptures, des surgissements de la discontinuité. C'est-à-dire qu'il s'agit d'une opération idéologique interne à la société, auto-opérée par ses propres sujets, et ayant pour but la préservation de la souveraineté (autrement dit la conservation de l'ordre hégémonique existant).

La réaction habituellement rencontrée au sein d'une société donnée, à la suite d'événements tels que des attentats terroristes importants, peut se résumer en un désir collectif, une nécessité même, de cohésion. Ces rassemblements populaires s'effectuent au sein du monde physique (sur les places des grandes villes comme sur les lieux de crime) autant que dans le monde numérique (sur les réseaux sociaux). Cette cohésion, ce regroupement, ce croisement d'intensités libidinales, représentent toujours *en soi* un potentiel danger pour l'ordre hégémonique existant, du simple fait qu'originairement, ils viennent d'*en bas*, émanant d'une « organisation » populaire imprévisible et difficile à contrôler. Dans la plupart des cas néanmoins, ce danger se trouve dissout sans intervention majeure des instances souveraines, et ce parce que les sujets sociaux ne cessent jamais, à l'exception de rares cas, de se comporter selon les préceptes de la *servitude volontaire*,[125] telle que La Boétie la décrit il y a presque cinq siècles. Ainsi, les intensités libidinales, que la cohésion a regroupées et renforcées, deviennent sujettes d'un abus, d'une réappropriation violente, mais paradoxalement, consensuelle. La cohésion glisse aisément de cette façon vers la coercition, tout en rétablissant ce que nous nommons ici confiance. Dès lors, cette coercition se joue sur les terrains linguistiques, politiques, axiologiques et ontologiques enfin, terrains dont il s'agira de proposer une cartographie.

Dans un souci de clarté, et avant d'accéder à l'objet central de notre étude, il nous faut d'abord exposer quelques repères théoriques au sujet de la notion de confiance. Il semble que la confiance soit aujourd'hui partout, sur toutes les lèvres: des hommes politiques fondent leurs campagnes électorales, leurs programmes, leurs lignes idéologiques sur la confiance (les « discours sécuritaires » en sont un exemple par excellence); des banques insistent sur ce terme dans leurs slogans publicitaires, pour séduire de

---

125 Voir Étienne de La Boétie, *Discours de la servitude volontaire* (Paris: Flammarion, 1993).

potentiels nouveaux clients; des life-coaches et des pseudopsychologues en font l'ingrédient principal d'une recette pour la vie heureuse. Plus sérieusement, un grand nombre de théories sociales considèrent la confiance comme un élément primordial et nécessaire au bon fonctionnement des sociétés. D'autre part, les théories économiques « orthodoxes » placent la confiance au cœur de leurs argumentations, expliquant grâce à elle des phénomènes tels que la monnaie ou encore les lois du marché. Cette liste pourrait s'étoffer et se voir approfondir, mais les deux exemples ici évoqués suffisent déjà à esquisser un aperçu de la place qu'occupe la notion de la confiance au sein des différents champs scientifiques.

Pour résister à ce genre de discours pragmatique, passe-partout, instrumentalisant, nous proposons de penser la confiance comme un système de principes, qui crée et renforce les relations de pouvoirs hégémoniques. Système de principes, ou plutôt « disposition des *archai* ». Cette dernière formulation semble plus précise, car l'*arché* grec (un terme cher à Giorgio Agamben entre autres) peut désigner aussi bien le « commencement » que le « commandement ».[126] Les *archai* de la confiance, ses origines perpétuelles, sont nombreuses et peuvent être ontologiques, psycho-sociales, économico-politiques, éthiques, cognitives et esthétiques, pour n'en nommer que quelques-unes.

Par leur omniprésence et leur omnipotence, ces *archai* s'avèrent non seulement régir tous les aspects de l'existence humaine, mais se trouvent parmi les facteurs primordiaux et déterminants du processus même d'anthropogenèse. De ce fait, il nous semble inconcevable de penser un monde sans croyance, sans crédit et sans confiance. Manipulateurs et dominants, les principes de la confiance sont donc fondamentaux et fondateurs de l'humanité telle qu'on la connaît, ou plutôt qu'on *croit* la connaître. Ainsi il convient de considérer la confiance elle-même comme un piège constituant et constitutif de l'humanité. Enfin, nous nommons l'homme qui ne peut exister et/ou subsister sans *croire en quelque chose* (ou même *croire être quelque chose*): *homo fidei*.

---

126 Voir Giorgio Agamben, *The Signature of All Things: On Method* (Brooklyn, NY: Zone books, 2009); et Agamben, *Qu'est-ce que le commandement?* (Paris: Payot & Rivages, 2013).

Il convient alors de se demander désormais, de quelle manière *nous sommes* piégés par la confiance, lorsque l'on dit, ou que l'on écrit par exemple, derrière un *hashtag* (« # »), sur un réseau social: « Je suis Charlie », « We are Orlando », « Nous sommes Bruxelles », etc., ou que nous déclarons plus généralement que « Nous sommes *quelque chose* » ?

Indiquons que du fait de l'instauration d'une identité entre « nous » et « quelque chose », un certain nombre de questions ontologiques se trouvent inévitablement posées. Référons-nous brièvement, pour aborder cette problématique, à la logique hégélienne, et plus précisément au livre premier de la *Science de la logique*[127] (communément nommé « grande Logique »), traitant de *l'être*. Chez Hegel, le « quelque chose » relève de la sphère de l'être, il est un *moment* de *l'être*, qui, considéré comme une immédiateté, représente une *positivité*, un *concret déterminé*, possédant ses *qualités* propres, etc. Une fois passé de la sphère de *l'être pur* à celle de *l'être-là*, ce *quelque chose* devient un *existant* et une *finité*. Ces déterminations sont-elles toutefois possibles *immédiatement* ? Hegel indique que toute immédiateté simple relève du caractère illusoire de l'être, et que même *quelque chose* apparaissant comme purement immédiate est en fait nécessairement le résultat d'une médiation. Tels questions appellent inévitablement à une confrontation avec le *travail du négatif*, et l'acceptation de négation comme seul moyen d'assurer la progression scientifique. Ces thèses centrales de la dialectique hégélienne, nous pouvons les résumer par une formule empruntée par l'auteur lui-même à Spinoza: « chaque détermination est une négation » (« *Omnis determinatio est negatio* »). Ainsi, le *quelque chose* doit non seulement être confronté à sa propre négativité dans la sphère de *l'être pur* (la réflexion intérieure), mais doit également, pour *passer dans l'être-là* et devenir un *étant*, être pris en compte à travers le prisme de la *réflexion extérieure* avec un *autre*. C'est précisément ce processus dynamique d'auto-dépassement qui constitue le *devenir*.

Ainsi, dire « Nous sommes Charlie », « Nous sommes Orlando », etc., *présuppose* un positionnement de ce *quelque chose* qu'*on est*, en opposition constitutive avec un *autre* (*autre* qui est à son tour *quelque chose*), que *nous ne sommes pas*. Le fonctionnement propre à la confiance vise cependant

---

[127] G. W. F. Hegel, *Science de la logique*, Livre I (Paris: Vrin, 2015).

à brouiller les pistes de ce processus d'auto-dépassement caractéristique au devenir, il tend à obscurcir le processus de « négation de la négation » (*Aufhebung*), afin de maintenir l'*illusion d'immédiateté*. La confiance revêt alors, pour parvenir à ces fins, la forme de son opposée la *méfiance*. Selon la dialectique hégélienne, la méfiance est « plus riche » que la confiance, car renfermant toutes les qualités de ce concept *premier* qu'elle a *relevé*, *dépassé* (« *aufgehoben* ») et étant de surcroît, munie d'un signe négatif. La méfiance donc, n'engendre pas l'absence de la confiance, un néant qui serait le résultat de sa négation abstraite, mais contient au contraire la confiance, et dispose grâce à son signe négatif (exprimé dans le langage par le préfixe *mé-*), d'une intensité persuasive plus grande encore.

Le piège fiduciaire mentionné plus haut, et dans lequel nous nous trouvons pris lorsque nous déclarons que « Nous sommes *quelque chose* », consiste donc en l'apparition d'un « nous » *méfiant*, affecté, ébranlé, un « nous » perturbé, détraqué même, et surtout fondamentalement identitaire, venu rétablir le sentiment fiduciaire d'appartenance. Un « nous » paranoïaque, pourrions-nous dire d'un point de vue psychanalytique, sans réduire les implications que cet état pathologique comporte (quels que soient ses divers définitions).[128] Ce « nous » se substitue dès lors à un amas d'individus, inconscients de leur propre « nous », incapables de se dire « nous » par eux-mêmes, ayant besoin d'une instance supérieure pour prononcer « nous » à leur place. Ce *nouveau* « nous », qui se manifeste comme réactionnaire, poursuit un unique but: refonder la confiance bousculée. Mais, de quelle façon?

Cette refondation fiduciaire se déroule majoritairement sur les voies onto-axiologiques. Dans le cas donné de #NousSommes, l'*être* et sa sous-catégorie les *valeurs* endossent le rôle de « principes » de la confiance. Ils interagissent, se substituent, changent de statut ontologique, tout cela afin de rétablir un consensus de valeurs et de préserver le statu quo social.

La poursuite de cette *arché*ologie de la confiance nécessite un examen ontologique du terme « nous », mot si familier semble-t-il, mais au

---

128   Pour rapprocher la notion de « méfiance » à celle « paranoïa », voir Sigmund Freud, *La naissance de la psychanalyse: lettres à Wilhelm Fliess, notes et plans, 1887–1902* (Paris: PUF, 1956), *Manuscrit H.* et *Manuscrit K.* notamment, ainsi que Jacques Lacan, *Les psychoses: 1955–1956* (Paris: Seuil, 1992).

potentiel cependant révolutionnaire, incitant à la défiance et à la subversion. Il conviendra ensuite de dresser une esquisse du statut ontologique que le « nous » acquiert, une fois placé dans le cadre fiduciaire du phénomène #NousSommes.

Il convient pour débuter de faire appel à la pensée de Jean-Luc Nancy, dont un segment important du travail se trouve, depuis des années, consacré à l'étude de la notion de communauté, et notamment aux divers et multiples sens que revêt le mot « nous ». Ainsi dans l'*Être singulier pluriel*, Nancy note que: « "nous" serait donc le préalable absolu, le plus reculé, de toute ontologie, et par conséquent "nous" serait aussi l'effet le plus tardif, le plus difficile, le moins appropriable, de l'exigence ontologique »[129]. Pour comprendre cette formule, il convient de tenir compte du fait que l'auteur, au sein de cette œuvre, et du reste comme lors de ses précédents travaux, tels que la *Communauté désœuvrée* ou la *Comparution*, a entrepris de renverser, en quelque sorte, l'ordre ontologique forgé par les discours dominants de la tradition philosophique occidentale. Qu'est-ce que cela signifie ?

Pour Nancy, *être-avec, être-en-commun*, ou encore *être-les-uns-avec-les-autres*, précède l'*être* même. Autrement dit, l'*être* est compris comme une disposition et non comme une présupposition (distinction qui constitue le point principal différenciant l'ontologie de Nancy à celle proposée par Hegel); ou mieux, l'*être* est compris à partir de l'*en*-commun et non « selon un être ou une essence du commun ».[130] Il est considéré comme co-originarité et co-existence et non comme une juxtaposition, une addition, un voisinage d'êtres soi-disant individuels, d'*ipséités* indépendantes et auto-originaires de leurs propres singularités solitaires. La co-ontologie proposée par Nancy exige ainsi une pensée « absolument et sans réserve à partir de l'*avec* ».[131] Une question simple se pose alors: comment caractériser cet *avec*? L'*avec* n'est « ni fond, ni sans fond », l'*avec* est la proximité éloignée, la simultanéité, la corrélation, la combinaison, le rapport, le croisement, le frôlement. Le seul présupposé de l'*avec* réside dans sa non-présupposition. Nancy va même plus loin, en écrivant que l'*avec* n'est *rien*, que l'*être* est cet

---

129 Jean-Luc Nancy, *Être singulier pluriel* (Paris: Galilée, 1996), p. 100.
130 Ibid., p. 76.
131 Ibid., p. 54.

« indicible », qui « ne peut pas être présenté comme un étant parmi les autres, puisque c'est le *parmi* même de tous les étant. Les singularités qui s'exposent et que cet *avec* dispose sont donc toujours déjà au pluriel ».[132]

Dans une telle constellation ontologique, « nous » n'avons besoin ni d'un Dieu ni d'un maître, pour dire « nous » à notre place. « Nous » est une scène sur laquelle nous *comparaissons*, chaque fois à nouveau et de manière inédite, pour nous identifier toujours à nouveau, et non pas au contraire pour nous rejoindre autour d'une identité d'ordre supérieur. Le « nous » est ainsi plutôt caractérisé par un processus de dés-identification.

Sur le plan axiologique maintenant, les valeurs qu'un tel « nous » produit ne sont jamais fondamentales, ne sont jamais substantielles, mais ne peuvent être que des *intensités* incommensurables traversant l'espace-temps simultané de l'*avec*. C'est là qui réside le trait subversif de la pensée de Nancy. Le « nous » est une *praxis* et un *ethos*. Mais, l'auteur nous met en garde, et affirme qu'on ne s'élève jamais à une hauteur suffisante pour dire « nous ». Le phénomène #NousSommes en est la preuve.

Chaque #NousSommes témoigne d'un désir irrépressible de « nous identifier en tant que "nous", en tant qu'un "nous" »[133] comme l'écrit Nancy. Toute pensée du « nous » constitue une pensée représentative et par ailleurs fiduciaire. Le « nous » repose toujours sur un concept, une idée, une notion, bref, sur ce qu'on nomme couramment une « valeur fondamentale ». Cette « valeur fondamentale » ne peut être comprise autrement que comme un *présupposé*. Par exemple, lorsque l'on dit que « Nous sommes Charlie », le « nous » se trouve créé de toutes pièces à partir de l'idée de « Charlie »; on pourrait aller plus loin en disant que le « nous » « repose » sur Charlie, c'est-à-dire sur les valeurs que Charlie représente, des universels, tels que la « laïcité » ou la « liberté d'expression », par exemple. C'est la même chose lorsque l'on dit « #Weareorlando »: le « nous » repose sur Orlando, qui dans son contexte, fait appel à et représente les valeurs engendrées par les droits LGBT, et plus largement se réfère en fait à l'universel des « droits de l'Homme ». Il a donc pour substance, ou devrait-on dire dès lors pseudo-substance, une valeur fondamentale pré-sup-posée. Tous ces suffixes, ces

---

132   Ibid., p. 110.
133   Ibid., p. 94.

termes ajoutés, accolés au #NousSommes, purement contextuels au premier abord, deviennent fondamentalement axiologiques et universalistes. Ils sont du reste des symptômes des manipulations onto-axiologiques ayant pour but de rétablir la confiance.

Cette pseudo-substantialisation des valeurs que nous venons d'examiner, semble se trouver au cœur du régime axiologique de la confiance. Tous les concepts, les notions, les idées contenues dans les termes accolés à #NousSommes conduisent à la réalisation, à la mise en œuvre de ce que Jean François Lyotard nomme dans son *Économie libidinale* le « grand Zéro ».[134] Ils sont les aboutissements d'un refroidissement des intensités, d'un retrait d'investissement, duquel résultent des concepts clairs et distincts, comme le concept de « liberté d'expression » pour Charlie, ou celui de « droits de l'Homme » pour Orlando. Des concepts qui se présentent comme des lieux autoproclamés de savoir, où *ceci* s'avère être distinctement différent de *cela*, où *ceci* n'est pas le *non-ceci*.

C'est sur ces valeurs se faisant passer pour des substances, sur ces pseudo-substances offrant une demeure temporaire aux « individus en détresse », que s'organisent les nouveaux « nous » réactionnaires, permettant de refonder la confiance. Le renversement, la substitution entre la substance et l'intensité attributive (intensité qui malgré son caractère errant, se laisse tôt ou tard apprivoiser), constitue le moteur de cette opération onto-axiologique de la confiance: le « nous » devient, paradoxalement, attribut de sa propre valeur. Pour reprendre l'exemple de Charlie, tout se passe comme si le « nous » devenait l'attribut de la « liberté d'expression », sans parvenir à s'assumer comme acteur d'une *expression libre*. Désormais pseudo-substantialisée, cette valeur perd tout son caractère intense. Dans le cas présent, le processus parait inversé: le « nous » fiduciaire a besoin de se fonder sur une valeur substantielle préétablie, fermement présupposée, façonnée par les forces dominantes. Ce positionnement onto-axiologique, représentant la fin du processus de pseudo-substantialisation de la valeur, et par là la refondation de la confiance, constitue précisément ce qui « nous » éloigne d'une quelconque forme d'entendement.

---

134 Jean-François Lyotard, *Économie libidinale* (Paris: Les éditions de Minuit, 1974), pp. 20–5.

Les passages d'intensités, même les plus bruyants, finissent ainsi par se taire. Beaucoup sont ceux qui préfèrent, par simple besoin de confort ou par soif de pouvoir, dévaloriser l'être-*en*-commun afin d'obtenir une valeur commune, ou plutôt, une valeur communément reconnue. Cette valeur commune qui nie l'être-en-commun, transforme tout être en quelque chose d'évaluable et toute existence en simple valorisation. Ainsi, l'entendement se trouve substitué par la croyance, et la vie est vécue à crédit. La valeur de pseudo-substance est ce socle monumental, sur lequel on monte solennellement pour ériger un « nous », mais ce à un prix ultime – la contrainte de devoir y rester, les chaînes attachées aux pieds, loin, dans un prétendu « au-dessus des *autres* », ces autres qui ne s'y trouvent pas, et ne l'atteindront jamais.

Et depuis ce piédestal, ou mieux, davantage encore sur ce piédestal, nous nous montrons toujours et uniquement à nous-mêmes. Nous nous trouvons, comme déjà se trouvaient les anciens Grecs, dans le théâtre de nos propres mythes. Comme le commente Jean-Luc Nancy, en se référant à Rousseau: nous sommes assemblés pour danser autour de l'arbre que nous avons planté afin d'en faire notre propre symbole. Pour Nancy: « il n'y a pas de société sans spectacle de la société ».[135] Le spectacle de la société est inévitable, mais peut néanmoins être bon, et alors « l'être social ou communautaire se présente sa propre intériorité, son origine, la fondation de son droit, la vie de son corps et la splendeur de son épanouissement ».[136] C'est le cas de la littérature, de la musique ou de l'art en général. En revanche, nous constatons l'ampleur de l'emprise de la confiance sur la coexistence, car beaucoup plus souvent, nous nous trouvons face à un spectacle mauvais où « l'être social se représente l'extériorité des intérêts et des appétits, les passions égoïstes et la fausse gloire de l'ostentation ».[137] Les exemples de ce mauvais spectacle sont innombrables, et le phénomène #NousSommes, malgré son apparence démocratique, spontanée et organique, en constitue l'un d'eux.

---

135 Jean-Luc Nancy, *Être singulier pluriel* (Paris: Galilée, 1996), p. 89.
136 Ibid., p. 90.
137 Ibid.

Ces quelques remarques sur la façon dont la confiance est refondée, d'un côté sur le plan ontologique, et de l'autre sur le plan axiologique, par le biais du phénomène #NousSommes, ces observations, ont été *intentionnellement* (avec une *intention sans intentions*) menées dans une visée d'accentuer l'urgence d'élaborer une pensée *défiante*; non pas une pensée « méfiante », car il s'agirait alors seulement d'une confiance au prétexte négatif. Une pensée qui tend, comme son adjectif le laisse deviner, à instaurer une mise-en-absence *essentielle* de la confiance, un retrait (ou un « re-trait »,[138] comme l'écrit Derrida) de la confiance, retrait qui ne provient ni de son *dehors*, ni de son *dedans*, catégories qui lui sont présupposées; mais qui au contraire représente un automouvement rétracteur de sa propre *limite*, une *réflexion limitrophe*. Ainsi la défiance lance un *défi* à la confiance. Et en déchiffrant les principes fiduciaires, la pensée défiante forme un courant menant à la dissolution même de la confiance, telle qu'esquissée avec cet exemple du #NousSommes.

À défaut de conclure, nous pouvons reprendre pour terminer les mots de Maurice Blanchot, cité par Nancy: « Le communisme: ce qui exclut (et s'exclut de) toute communauté déjà constituée ».[139] Cette définition, pourrait être paraphrasée, adaptée à notre propos, donnant ainsi: la défiance: ce qui exclut (et s'exclut) de toute opinion déjà constituée. En ce sens, la défiance devrait aller par-delà tout désir persistant d'une communauté, et même par-delà tout désir persistant d'une opinion commune.

Enfin, en empruntant quelques cheminements de la pensée de Derrida (qui s'appuie également sur l'œuvre de Blanchot) il faudrait encore ajouter que la défiance réclame une alliance sans institution ni appartenance, une alliance qui n'est ni automatique ni naturelle, une alliance sans communauté, une communauté sans communauté. « X sans X », la formule par laquelle « le même mot et la même chose paraissent enlevés à eux-mêmes, soustraits à leur référence et à leur identité, tout en continuant de se laisser traverser, dans leur vieux corps, vers un tout autre en eux dissimulé ».[140] Désormais

---

138 Pour connaître le sens précis que Derrida donne au terme « re-trait », voir Jacques Derrida, *Parages* (Paris: Galilée, 1985).

139 Jean-Luc Nancy, *La communauté désœuvrée* (Paris: Christian Bourgeois, 1986), p. 25.

140 Jacques Derrida, *Parages* (Paris: Galilée, 1985), p. 84.

scruté à travers le prisme de la défiance, le « nous » apparaît comme un lien intempestif, sans statut; comme un lieu discret, secret presque, pourrait dire Derrida, ne possédant ni nom ni titre, sans partie ni patrie, sans co-citoyenneté, sans appartenance commune à une classe et sans rassemblement assuré. Et finalement, ce « nous » défiant se trouve aussi sans opinions communes, sans convictions préétablies, et sans valeurs fondamentales. Il pourrait alors être tentant de se demander si la défiance n'est pas peut-être, au fond, une confiance sans confiance, son *degré zéro*.

Bibliographie

Agamben, Giorgio, *Qu'est-ce que le commandement?*, trad. Joël Gayraud (Paris: Payot & Rivages, 2013).
——, *The Signature of All Things: On Method*, trad. Luca D'Isanto et Kevin Atell (New York: Zone Books, 2009).
de La Boétie, Étienne, *Discours de la servitude volontaire* [1576] (Paris: Flammarion, 1993).
Debord, Guy, *La Société du spectacle* [1967] (Paris: Gallimard, 1996).
Derrida Jacques, *Parages* (Paris: Galilée, 1985).
Freud, Sigmund, *La naissance de la psychanalyse: lettres à Wilhelm Fliess, notes et plans, 1887–1902*, trad. Anne Berman (Paris: PUF, 1956).
Hegel, G. W. F., *Science de la logique: Livre premier, l'être* [1812], trad. B. Bourgeois, (Paris: Vrin, 2015).
Lacan, Jacques, *Les psychoses: 1955–1956* (Paris: Seuil, 1992).
Lyotard, Jean-François. *Économie libidinale* (Paris: Les éditions de Minuit, 1974).
Nancy, Jean-Luc, *Être singulier pluriel* (Paris: Galilée, 1996).
——, *La communauté désœuvrée* (Paris: Christian Bourgeois, 1986).

#NousSommes and Automatic Politics: An Interview with Martin Crowley[141]

One of the key problematics that you have been developing, Martin, is that of automatic politics: how are you understanding this term? Moreover, what are the specific political problems that come with automation?

MARTIN CROWLEY: So, probably a helpful way to come at that would be through the second half: specific political problems that come with automation, inasmuch as that's a problematic that's very much to the fore in the guise of the social policy and economic question of the consequences of generalised, widespread automation of labour. Some of the more catastrophic of the predictions around this area predict up to 50 per cent of jobs to be lost in Western post-industrial economies as a result of the automation of labour; other predictions are much lower than that. Regardless, there does seem to be a consensus amongst those who have studied these questions that in the coming two decades this is going to be a significant issue, and if it's an issue, this is partly, of course, because of the role of paid employment in constructing a sense of participation in social processes and so on, but also, and more specifically in economic terms, because a collapse in employment of that scale would bring with it a collapse in purchasing power and, given that the economy in the areas in question is an economy founded predominantly on consumption, a collapse in purchasing power would be truly disastrous. Hence suggestions along the lines of a universal basic income, for example, as one way of addressing that scenario; so you would, for instance, have a specific tax on profits generated by that

---

141 Conducted by Susie Cronin, Sofia Ropek Hewson and Cillian Ó Fathaigh on Monday, 30 April 2018, in Cambridge.

rise in automation, which would be used in order to provide a universal basic income. Now, if I have taken that as a way in, it's because that question of a universal basic income gets us to questions of what we think the relation between human beings and their technologies is or ought to be, and how we ought to think about that relation. So, one of the most common versions of that UBI scenario such as you find in Nick Smicek and Alex Williams' *Inventing the Future*, for example, effectively revives a bit of Marx and the idea that under communism, because labour will no longer be organised in the interests of its exploitation, this will free up time for creative, fulfilling activity of various sorts, and so the version of this scenario that we find, not only in Smicek and Williams' book, though paradigmatically there, is that the machines will save us all this time that we would have spent labouring, which will be freed up for more creative, enjoyable pursuits. Now, what I am interested in there specifically would be the relation between human beings and their technology in that scenario, because that version of relations between human beings and their technology maintains a scenario in which technology – the instrument – is a useful instrument that mediates the relationship between human beings and their world. And this is where we can start to transition from something like the politics of automation to more questions about the relation between automation and politics: if we were to start to look not just at what kind of policy we might have to develop in relation to automation, but how automation is affecting politics, we might start to see how a human relation to technology in general is poorly captured, shall we say, by the notion of instrumentality. One thing that we could think of is everything that has been in the news of late about the role of very fine-grained user profiling in social media in relation to electoral politics. This is one thing that shows that the technology is not just a tool that is then deployed by more or less well-meaning human actors for more or less sinister ends: rather, the technical form itself already opens possibilities of action and interaction that simply previously did not exist, and the politics of that scenario then has to do with the conjoint action of, let's call them 'assemblages', in which particular social groups meet particular economic interests, meet particular financial instruments, and so on – and meet particular technologies, obviously. The whole of that forms an assemblage, and it's the assemblage that produces the distinctive form of action in question. We can unpack that thinking about Cambridge Analytica, Facebook, offshore funding, Brexit, etc.: this is the sort of assemblage that I have in mind. And the kind of action that is going on there, it seems to me, can only fully be understood if we see it as an action produced by the collaboration of all those different factors. Again because, let's say, if we think about the financial instruments concerned, then the speed of the technologies involved, for example, provides forms of invisibility or semi-visibility in relation to existing legal frameworks. So clearly it is not enough to think of technology as a tool in that case, since it clearly has a constitutive role in producing the form of action in question. So what then becomes particularly interesting for me in that scenario is wondering whether there are ways of thinking about agency and specifically political agency that can account for that kind of conjoint assemblage-level action whilst retaining the possibility of decisive, interventionist models of activity, rather than simply reducing to post facto descriptions of how these processes have taken place. Broadly speaking, that question of whether there are types of sharp, incisive, prescriptive political agency that can be understood as operative through these kinds of ontologically plural assemblages. That for me would be the question posed by that concept of automatic politics.

How does this concept of automatic politics relate to teleology? The accounts that you've described all seem to assume that there will be a certain end-point in the future that will free up labour. Is your way of describing an 'agency' that can operate in the moment with a specific assemblage a counter to that teleology?

MARTIN CROWLEY: I think that that teleological dimension is absolutely connected to what is conceptually a metaphysical separation between the human and the machine in that thinking. And so in that sense, the machine essentially becomes a resource through which the human will come fully to develop itself in some way. And, again, that instrumental relation seems to me to miss ways in which the operation of technical forms is already constitutive of modes of human existence and forms of human possibility and so on. And we could also wonder about the question of teleology also slightly differently, because one thing that thinking about agency as distributed across assemblages of different actors in this way does do is severely problematise models of agency in terms of intentionality. And that then does become quite difficult in terms of trying to think about this politically. In one sense, what I'm trying to think in this work is the possibility of a conception of agency that does imply the possibility of taking a strong position, which would be an interventionist position, without that being made possible by and solely by a prior conceptualisation of a desired outcome on the part of a human being who then decides how best to realise that outcome. In a sense then this is an attempt to understand a strongly decisive conception of political agency in a fully processual ontology, epistemology and so on. And that's not straightforward, but there are people who can help us do that: Stiegler is one of them, and the later work of Guattari is also very helpful in those terms.

Much of your analysis involves an engagement and elaboration of the work of Bernard Stiegler, but also philosophers like Gilbert Simondon. What do you feel French philosophy has to offer this issue?

MARTIN CROWLEY: I think first of all we would have to approach this via a number of fairly hefty qualifications. So, I'm not sure necessarily that French philosophy as such has anything more to offer on this issue than all manner of other forms of thought and practice. There are important ways of coming at these issues through media theory for example, through people like Friedrich Kittler or Yves Citton, so I'm not sure that philosophy (whether French or not) has anything preeminent to offer here. I certainly don't think that if only we could get the thinking right then everything would follow: I am absolutely persuaded that that's not how it works. That said, what the French thinkers who I've found helpful in this kind of area – more specifically Latour, Stiegler, Malabou, but also as you say, Simondon, and also Citton, actually – what I think they do offer is, on the one hand, a commitment to thinking about these kinds of issues absolutely in the midst of their social and political urgency whilst at the same time – and this is where a more, let's say 'critical' dimension comes in – suspending certain of the concepts that we might usually use to help us think about these kinds of problems. So we might think for example of the way in which Stiegler places in suspension or withdraws any kind of precritical conception of the human in his work. So, as I've been saying, I don't think we're going to get very far in these questions if we start by assuming that we know what a human being is, we know what a technical form is, or a form of technology is, and all we've got to do now is work out how one relates to another. That gesture of disqualifying some of our more familiar terms of reference in relation to these arguments has the great advantage, I think, of allowing us to explore and then if appropriate to understand the extent to which the processes that we feel it's urgent to analyse are themselves already displacing, shifting, or rendering inoperative, some of those key terms of reference. So, as I say, I don't believe that that in itself is a preeminent offering and nor do I want to persuade you that it's only these frameworks that are offering that. But a critical, conceptual approach to these issues, whilst understanding that this is being practised in the midst of social and political urgency, that in itself seems to me to offer possibilities of insight and incisiveness that are not offered by all approaches, let's say.

One of the major problems that we have seen with the internet, but especially social media, is that it has presented itself as a site of violence against marginalised groups in society, and perhaps especially women. Do you think there is space within the work of thinkers like Stiegler, to accommodate this issue?

MARTIN CROWLEY: Yes, I certainly do. And partly that would link to what I was just saying in my response to the previous question inasmuch as that willingness to suspend, withdraw, or critique existing terms of reference means that an approach to these questions of, broadly speaking, the politics of technology, let's say, those kind of questions, necessarily will take a critical approach to the way in which concepts, figures, forms of subjectivation and so on are being practised and wielded in these areas. It also offers the possibility of understanding the ways in which particular technical forms offer the possibility of understanding new inflections of old forms of oppression and violence, for example, and also make new forms of oppression and violence possible. But also crucially how these produce new forms of subjectivation and new subject positions therefore through those processes. I think it's important to understand – for example, thinking of Jon Ronson's book *So You've Been Publicly Shamed*, it may be that the subject position of having had your life destroyed through social media shaming is itself something else – a wholly new mode of subjectivation. The constellation of affects, social relations, the physical, emotional, psychological relation with the technological forms in question – all of those things are entirely specific to that mode and so, understanding ways in which forms of technology can constitute modes of subjectivation or modes of interaction and so on offers the possibility of a really detailed attention to the nature and quality of the experiential quality of the existential stakes of these forms of interaction. Some of this is extremely everyday – it is the kind of thing we discuss every day. The kinds of hostility, particularly in terms of misogyny, made possible via the kinds of invisibility permitted by these modes of technology: we are very familiar with that, but it is still very easy to talk about it as a tool that allows a person to do this or that. It's actually much more productive to understand that the misogynistic troll is a new mode of subjectivation; understanding exactly what is the composite of affects, social relations, technological competence or otherwise, and so on, that structures that mode of subjectivation. That, I think, gets us much further in thinking about what is going on in those forms of violence, for example. But it's also important to understand that various of these modes make possible modes of protest and forms of liberation that again have their specificity, and have their specificity in the relation they display between various contemporary technical forms, particularly in terms of social media and existing social and technical forms in terms of public space, legislation, forms of public address and so on. So if you think of either #MeToo or #BlackLivesMatter, both of those can be defined – to an extent – by the novelty of the relation between discourse, state forms, industry norms and protocols, the occupation of public space and public visibility, the speed and ease of solidarity, the relation to older forms of manifestation such as mass demonstrations, the relation to existing forms of civil society, to existing structures and forms of lawmaking, and so on. In a way, thinking of the expanded field, we can think about ways in which forms of social conflict and social struggle are being reconfigured and new forms invented through the assemblages into which some of these newer technical forms are playing.

Stiegler has written that we need the proliferation of new economies of contribution centred on systems of 'care': how do you think Stiegler's conception of care is constituted (through race, gender, vulnerability?), and how does it relate to the politics of automation, if it does?

MARTIN CROWLEY: Probably the major framework in relation to which Stiegler's conception of care is elaborated is intergenerationally: so the subtitle of *Taking Care*, as it's translated in English, is 'Of the Generations,' and if that's the case it's because for Stiegler the relation between generations is organised by technical forms. The most fundamental point for Stiegler about technics is that the form of life called 'human' is defined for him by the role of technical forms in transmitting memory from generation to generation – and that memory is transmitted impersonally through technical forms. Now, at that point the relation to questions of politics of automation, I think, is reasonably clear, because then the question becomes what forms of transmission and what forms of relation are constituted through the operation of and relation to the particularity of forms. More broadly though, Stiegler makes, I think, very helpful use of Amartya Sen's concept of capabilities – although as this makes its way into Stiegler's French as *capacités/capacitation*, it then makes its way into Stiegler's English, as it were, as capacities, capacitation, as well as capabilities. The key point in that is that capabilities are not in some sense given, that capabilities are socially distributed – they are socially distributed goods. So if we want to think about new economies and contribution to care, for example particularly if we want to think of the politics of forms of automation in relation to questions of race, gender, vulnerability, and so on, I think it's extremely interesting to look at what Stiegler does with that idea of capabilities as socially distributed goods, inasmuch as for Stiegler the distribution of those capabilities is precisely what is effected by modes of relation to and interaction with technical forms, modes of adoption of technical forms. So at that point, as there already is the question of distribution of capabilities, that is obviously a political question – but it means that that political question is already a question of the politics of technology: how are engagement with and participation in the technical forms distributed, what is the pattern of distribution of those modes across a given social field and how is that distribution differentiated, and so on. That mapping, those differentials, then become crucial: the mode in which a technical form is adopted by individuals and collectivities gives us quite a fine-grained way of thinking about the politics in question. So it is not simply that group A has better access to a given technology than group B: it's that at a particular time, the structure of our existence is produced in collaboration with the defining technical forms of that existence *and* then there is also the properly political question of the ways in which those technical forms are adopted by different groups. This is where Stiegler builds in a recursive dimension to the interaction with technical forms. Since we are existentially, cognitively, physically, in all sorts of ways defined with our technical forms, the structures of our decision-making, for example, therefore cannot be understood as if they were in some sense ahistorical or transcendent in relation to these technical forms. We still do have decisions to take, though. It is not as if Stiegler is preaching some sort of determinism here at all – it's not that in the least, it's a question of constitution, yes, and a moment of decision on the mode of adoption. And that adoption is socially and conflictually distributed, so the broader political question becomes to do with that: how are these technical forms to be adopted and how is that adoption mapped onto the fault lines within a particular social field.

When you first described automatic politics, you made a distinction between the purely financial and a sense of participation in the social process, but also how that participation is distributed. Within that, is there a distinction between a sense of participation and participation itself, that is one as a more holistic engagement and the other as something more derivative?

MARTIN CROWLEY: That opens what is, in some ways, a tricky question in relation to Stiegler. Namely the extent to which he has to valorise some forms of experience as more 'authentic' than others. Given that he develops Simondon's concept of *proletarianisation*, for example, and that concept is itself derived from Marx, that concept may be carrying through a model of alienation as its basic grammar. And this comes through again in the work that Stiegler has done on the automation of labour, and the difference between labour and work, where work is the valorised term. Precisely because work is what, for him, permits forms of individuation, and so it is curative, constructive, productive, and so on. So there is arguably the risk that we can slip here into thinking that there is something like good forms of activity and degraded forms of activity. Crucially, what Stigler will say is that actually it is useful and important to think in terms of distinctions between what is helpful and unhelpful, what is – to use the classic opposition from the *pharmakon* – what is curative and what is poisonous. We can do that without having to think in terms of degradation or in terms of any kind of falling off from something authentic. Stiegler would use Nietzsche and say that he is thinking about it in tragic terms, which is to say that everything is always a composition of the good and the bad. And then it is a question of which tendency one seeks to promote. So, in that sense, I think we can say, if we think about participation, then we can think of the two versions of participation that you described as two tendencies and the promotion of one or the other is precisely where the political dimension comes in. Is the form of participation that is being promoted through the way in which this technical form is being adopted, is that form of participation likely to prove beneficial or not? We don't have to measure beneficial in relation to some gold standard of authentic experience, we can simply measure it in terms of what is experienced as opening existential possibilities and so on. So, I think the way to do it is not as an opposition, but as a composition, as Stiegler would say, of tendencies and then the political question, through the mode of adoption, becomes which tendencies are being promoted, and where, and for and with whom and so on.

In terms of agency, in your view, to what extent is there a possibility of selectivity in terms of different models of engagement and use of the internet? For instance, in terms of using Gmail and being obliged to accept all the terms and conditions, etc. Do you believe there are alternative models which could provide greater agency to internet users, and in relation to technology more generally?

MARTIN CROWLEY: There clearly are alternative models, in that these exist: they are out there and are being practised. One can think of various instances, of which Shareware is one of the more obvious examples. The question, to my mind – and again we can frame this in terms of the politics of capabilities and their distribution – in terms of the possibility of alternative models here the question is not whether these exist but rather who is capable of discovering these and enjoying their benefits. So partly again that's a question of the distribution of capabilities as social goods (here in the mode of what we might rapidly call digital literacy, by which I would mean a functional understanding of the role of the operation of the technologies in question), and also – and this is where the economics comes in initially – a critical understanding of the way in which these technologies are embedded in existing economic relations and, for the most part, serving these. The second way in which the economic question comes in then is precisely that – there are reasons why these alternative models bringing with them that critical digital literacy are not that widespread, and that reason is quite straightforwardly to do with profit motive, monopoly, platform capitalism and so on. Again, what I think we have to hold on to here is that, let's say, the model of one's participation in the use of online technologies, for example, that needs to be a model in which we understand that participation in the use of online technologies is itself a mode of subjectivation defined by its embedding in a particular set of relations to human and non- human actors and factors. And, to be as nuanced about it as possible, what I think we have to be looking at is the ways in which differential relations to models of participation are also differentially organising modes of subjectivation. So, as I say, the technological question is what models are there and how they can be developed. The political question is what modes of subjectivation are produced through the differentially distributed participation in these models. That is what, I think, we find ourselves bumping up against in the questions posed by the quasi-monopolies that have come to exist in relation to many of these technologies, as shown by your example of the Gmail terms and conditions.

How do you believe this phenomenon of automation, in relation to the internet, has impacted conceptions of personhood? It seems, in a sense, that the traditional conception of identity has become detached from the physical or the material, by, for instance, the creation of online avatars on social media?

MARTIN CROWLEY: I think emphasis on the physical and the material is extremely helpful in relation to this. Initially of course because the function of the avatar and the experience of using an avatar can be understood through an idea of dematerialisation, in a sense, and that's precisely one of the things that produces the cloak of invisibility as an invitation to modes of incivility and hostility and so on. But one thing I think that we can see going on here will be that conceptions of personhood, selfhood, or subjectivity, whatever we have understood by those terms has always meant in fact something that is produced collaboratively across various different modes of embodiment and relation. Thinking of the question of the avatar to start with, then: for me the critical thing in the idea of identity or mode of subjectivation generated in part by the operation of that kind of technical form is to think of that as some kind of composite whole rather than an abstract or immaterial subjectivity. For example, to think its affective, racial, gendered, economic dimensions and so on as intersectionally as we possibly can, and to understand the technical form itself as part of that intersection. But if we map this back it's not particularly helpful to think that the technologies in question are themselves in some sense immaterial. That is plainly not true, and forgetting their materiality is again a way to forget the politics of differential distribution of capabilities and so on, in the way that we have been thinking about these. We might think, for example, of the racial politics of social housing policy in relation to power lines, to remember the materiality that defines these supposedly immaterial technologies. So there is nothing immaterial either about the technologies or about the modes of subjectivation in question – there is very little that is more material than the kind affective intensities that are at work within the social media troll while trolling or being confronted in the person being trolled. But the materiality is distributed, something like selfhood or subjectivity is distributed there through bodies, machines, spaces of social relation, forms of equipment, financial instruments again, and so on. Oddly, perhaps, remembering the materiality of forms and what they generate is also a way of remembering that something like subjectivity always was material and technical and distributed and relational in any event. Interiority, psychological or subjective interiority is something that is produced in intimate relation to particular technical forms, not least the technical form of printing. That form of psychological interiority was itself already the product of a network of different, more or less material factors, and not just the product but was co-producing itself with that network of different factors.

At the advent of the internet, there was perhaps a utopic understanding of its potential, with ideas such as 'Cyberdemoracy'; how do you believe this has changed, particularly in light of phenomena such as cyberattacks and fake news, and probably at this point Cambridge Analytica now also?

MARTIN CROWLEY: There is a sense in which the miserable or disastrous dimension of the way in which some of these recent developments are taken up or the way in which these circulate is extremely salutary – I certainly do agree that some of those ways of thinking about the potential of the internet were plainly utopian and it's of course instructive that some of the most enthusiastic boosters of those utopian notions who indeed continue to promote them in utopian terms are exactly those agents who are profiting most – not just in financial terms but also in terms of social power from the way in which these technologies have developed and have become socially embedded. So it is obviously now a lot easier to be sceptical about these things than it might have been at one point. That is clearly a good thing. What I think the negativity of the ways in which some of these developments have been received and circulate – what that absolutely flags up is the inseparability of technical forms from the broader assemblages of which they form a part. The question of cyberattacks, let's say, is incomprehensible if we are not thinking in terms of technical forms, state apparatuses, more or less concealed geopolitical rivalry and very local effects of group formation, and so on. You can't think cyberattacks without thinking of different networks or assemblages of different actors and factors. And then what we have to try to understand then is how a specific form of geopolitical agency is being produced through the interaction of those different actors and factors. It's a very good example of how that agency is absolutely decisionistic and interventionistic, and decisive, without being reducible to simply the malign putting into practice of some sort of evil plan – however much we might be tempted by its reporting to think of it in those terms. By which I don't mean at all that there is nothing malign about some of these activities – but that the way in which these activities might be malign or benign has to be understood in terms of the nature of the activity itself and not in terms of a speculative projection as to the mentality of some alleged author.

We have to understand that politics – the politics of these activities – can only be understood in terms of the full range of networks through which and across which the agency in question develops. So, in one sense we find ourselves at the sharp end of what had at one point been promoted at the very least as considerably cuddlier than this. But in a way all that is is a reminder that technical forms participate in assemblages with all other sorts of other factors. Which is certainly not to say that there is nothing to be concerned about – it's to say that what we have to be concerned about will be specific to *this* assemblage. There were things to be concerned about in the operation of the telegraph, for example, or the laying of telegraph cables under the Atlantic, and the safety of these. This doesn't mean there is nothing specific or concerning in a new assemblage, but there is no way of understanding what might be concerning if we insist on considering it as in some sense utterly unprecedented.

In L'Université sans condition *(2001), Jacques Derrida speaks about the effect of the internet and the virtual on the university space specifically: do you believe that there has been such a change and how does this relate to our potential for political activity?*

MARTIN CROWLEY: Probably the most obvious effect of the Internet on university teaching, if we think about it globally, is the development of massive, open online courses – and the thing to observe there, I think, is just how little the possibilities of the technology in question are being thought about in its deployment in that pedagogical mode. By which I mean that it's a great thing obviously to be able to access all kinds of teaching remotely – there is no reason to think that that's a bad thing in itself – but what is significant for our purposes here is the way in which the role of the technology has been to simply offer a further opportunity to the marketised university. In that sense, the role and the possibilities of the technologies itself are *not there* in that example, they're adopted just as a way of enhancing what was going to be done anyway, even more effectively, even more efficiently. We could see something similar, I think, in much of what goes on under the name of the Digital Humanities: for example, where the role of the 'digital' in the digital humanities is often either to provide new forms of illustration, which offer new possibilities of access and understanding and manipulability and so on, or through large-scale data gathering to permit the humanities to return to the mode of positivism. The challenge, I think (and this ought to be evident from what I have been saying about distribution of capabilities and modes of subjectivation and so on) – the challenge is to understand the way in which the digital opens possibilities: forms of thinking and therefore discussion, debate, ways of existing as a learner, ways of existing as a teacher, can be newly generated. Now, obviously, that's why in one way I started by saying that I don't necessarily mean that all MOOCs are bad and wrong in and of themselves: these are generative of modes of teaching and learning that did not previously exist, and there's no reason to think that some of those might not be enormously beneficial in some cases. But the mistake again is simply to understand the technology as a tool. What we need to understand is the way in which the technology itself is already reconfiguring what we thought our activity was: that's why I don't think it's good enough simply to think that this technology will allow you to do an enhanced version of what you could do before. When I am, for example, sitting with a group of students, discussing a particular topic and those students are searching for information about that topic in real time and feeding that into the discussion, that is a different relation – on the part of all of us in that scenario – that is a different relation to something we might call knowledge and the temporality of knowledge. How knowledge is being produced in that discussion, then, becomes very differently structured to what would have been the case a generation ago. And so again, how the participants in that discussion are developing their own roles in relation to that knowledge is also changing significantly, as is what it means to be a participant in that scenario, which is to say, that form of subjectivation. What's more, the object of the exercise is not in some sense ahistorical, unchanging eternally, as if there were something called 'knowledge' that has always existed and will always exist – whatever is being produced in a discussion such as that is being produced along with its participants and along with the technology in question, again it is a co-production and collaboration on the part of all of those elements, which includes knowledge as it used to be, which is also being inflected and is in play here. We have to understand that who we think we are, what we think we're doing, what we think we're dealing with in these processes: all that is being generated through those processes in very different ways.

Our focus in this collection is to engage with questions of collectivity and the digital, via the theme of #NousSommes. Do you believe there has been a change in our conception of the collective in the online space? Or have much of these phenomena, such as 'echo chambers' already existed historically?

MARTIN CROWLEY: I think there certainly has been a change in the ways that we conceive of the collective, although mostly I think that change has been to do with the emergence of new kinds of human collective enabled by online space. And mostly we would think of those in terms of the ways in which online users are relating to each other and forming new kinds of collectives that might not have existed previously. The emphasis in the way we tend to discuss these things is in how collectives may be formed without people ever meeting each other 'IRL' (in real life) – and that is already a very good example of how modes of subjectivation are co-producing themselves along with these forms of technology. What I'd like to emphasise, though, is rather that one thing we see through such phenomena is the emergence of collectives – which are collective not only in the sense of being a group of human beings but which are collective in the sense of a group of ontologically diverse actors and factors. I already referred earlier to #BlackLivesMatter and #MeToo as examples of exactly that – we could alternatively think of Anonymous, whose name takes that idea of an existential mode that has been co-produced by those human individuals and the technical forms with which they are working. This is one of the interesting things in their use of the Guy Fawkes mask from *V for Vendetta*: the role of the mask in Alan Moore's graphic novel and then in the film is not the role of the mask as it appears in the interventions of

Anonymous. This is something like anonymity but as a new mode of political intervention: it is not simply humans actors deploying these tools to produce that intervention, but rather the nature of the intervention is itself new and absolutely structured by effects of temporality, again, effects of speed, but also by effects of geographical distribution, both on the part of human participants and on the part of the corporations, for example, into which they might be intervening. All of the structures that are at work there are defined only by their participation in the assemblage in question.

And so that is what I mean in saying that the form of action in question is distinct from anything else that might be practised elsewhere by other conjoint forms of agency.

So, we can always think about these possibilities as new inflections of modes or forms that have existed previously, and in many cases they are, but what I think some of these more recent developments have encouraged us to understand is the way in which forms of intervention, let's say, are practised by already plural collectivities of actors and factors, and that arguably is a new sense not only of political agency but of what it is that we understand by the idea of a collective in the broadest sense.

Notes on Contributors/Notes sur les auteurs

BENOÎT LE BOUTEILLER a été éducateur, chef de service et directeur de plusieurs établissements sociaux et médicaux sociaux en France. Il est aujourd'hui psychanalyste au Brésil.

MARIE CHABBERT is an AHRC doctoral candidate and stipendiary lecturer at the University of Oxford. Her thesis, which focuses on the work of Georges Bataille, Jacques Derrida, Gilles Deleuze and Jean-Luc Nancy, is entitled 'Faithful Deicides: Contemporary French Thought and Religion After the Death of God'. Her recent publications include chapters in monographs published by Routledge, Peter Lang and Les Presses Universitaires de Nanterre. She is also co-editing a special issue of *Angelaki: Journal of the Theoretical Humanities* and a Routledge monograph on the work of Jean-Luc Nancy.

JACK COOPEY is a PhD German candidate at Durham University. His doctoral work concerns the concept of totality from Kant to Derrida (2016–2019) in Fredric Jameson, supervised by Gerald Moore. He read English Literature and History at the University of Leicester (2012–2015). While there, he worked with Ian Harris on a dissertation on Locke and the State of Nature, which consolidated his interest in the philosophy of history and literature. After his bachelor's degree, he undertook a Master's of Letters in Intellectual History at the University of St Andrews (2015–2016), working with Caroline Humfress on essays concerning Derrida, Badiou's and Nietzsche's Saint Paul, and a master's thesis on Foucault in the Collège de France lectures.

MARTIN CROWLEY is Reader in Modern French Thought and Culture at the University of Cambridge, where he is also Anthony L. Lyster Fellow and Director of Studies in Modern and Medieval Languages at Queens' College. His publications include *Duras, Writing and the Ethical* (Oxford University Press, 2000), *Robert Antelme: Humanity, Community,*

Testimony (Legenda, 2003), and *L'Homme sans: Politiques de la finitude* (Lignes, 2009; afterword by Jean-Luc Nancy). He is also General Editor of the journal *French Studies*. He is presently completing a book project, entitled *The Accidental Agent: Politics without Transcendence in Latour, Stiegler and Malabou*. This examines the possibility of an effective, decisive politics which would not rely on human exceptionalism, through consideration of this question in the work of Bruno Latour, Bernard Stiegler and Catherine Malabou and case studies of contemporary political scenarios.

MARIANNE GODARD est une étudiante en littérature française à l'université McGill. Sa recherche se centre sur les problématiques du corps et les rapports à l'altérité dans la littérature française des 20e et 21e siècles.

ALEXANDRE LESKANICH is a PhD student in the School of Modern Languages, Literatures and Cultures, Royal Holloway, University of London. He holds a BA and an MA in History from the University of Leicester, an MSc in Philosophy from the University of Edinburgh, and an MSc in Political Theory from the London School of Economics and Political Science. His work has appeared or is forthcoming in *Rethinking History: The Journal of Theory and Practice*, *Journal of the Philosophy of History*, *Critical Inquiry*, *European Review of History: Revue européenne d'histoire*, *Philosophy in Review*, *Dějiny – Teorie – Kritika* [*History – Theory – Criticism*] and *The English Historical Review*.

PATRICIA MACCORMACK is Professor of Continental Philosophy at Anglia Ruskin University and publishes on feminism, queer theory, posthumanism, horror films, animal rights, cinesexuality and ethics. Her publications include *The Animal Catalyst* (edited anthology, Bloomsbury, 2014), *Posthuman Ethics* (Ashgate, 2012) and *Cinesexuality* (Ashgate, 2008).

SOLANGE MANCHE is a PhD student in French at the University of Cambridge. Her doctoral thesis looks into the (re-)emergence of the critique of political economy in contemporary philosophy, after the 2008 economic crisis. More specifically, she explores the potential of the work of Catherine Malabou, Bernard Stiegler, and Frédéric Lordon to grasp post-crash transindividuation.

ANDREA PERUNOVIC, né à Belgrade (Serbie) en 1989, est Docteur en Philosophie et Littérature française (Université Paris 8, France – thèse soutenue: « Archéologie de la confiance: prolégomènes d'une pensée défiante ») et doctorant en Philosophie, Art, et Pensée critique (European Graduate School, Suisse).

BOUBÉ YACOUBA SALIFOU est doctorant en philosophie des normes au Centre Atlantique de Philosophie (Université Rennes 1). Il est aussi un enseignant-vacataire en méthodologie de l'information à l'Université de Nantes, ainsi qu'enseignant-vacataire en philosophie à l'Université Abdou Moumouni, Niger. Il est également membre du comité de rédaction de la revue Philosophie et Sciences Sociales, *Nazari*.

Index

agency 3, 5, 7, 75, 83, 143–4, 149, 152–3, 156
Anthropocene 4–5, 6–7, 27, 29, 34, 36, 55, 59, 62–71
Arendt, Hannah 28–9, 37, 64, 108–9
assemblages 92, 143, 153, 156

Bataille, Georges 13
Benjamin, Walter 7, 76–8, 80–4
Bolsonaro, Jair 110–11, 115
Bookchin, Murray 28–9, 31–6, 38
Braidotti, Rosi 27–8, 30, 32, 38

Charlie Hebdo 1, 7, 42, 50–2, 85–7, 94, 95, 98
collective 1, 4, 7–8, 15, 35, 38, 51, 75, 77, 84, 87, 90, 102, 155–6
community 1, 4–5, 7–8, 15, 27, 29, 31, 33, 75–6, 82
cyberattacks 152
cyberdemocracy 3

Deleuze, Gilles 9–13, 16, 18, 21, 105
Derrida, Jacques 8, 18, 138–9, 153
digital 1–5, 7–8, 18, 75, 109, 114, 150, 154, 155

Enlightenment, the 28, 78, 80
ethics 6, 9, 19, 21, 31–3, 36

Facebook 103, 110, 113, 114, 143
film 5, 62, 115, 155

hashtags 1, 3, 4, 6, 75, 132
Hegel, Georg Wilhelm Friedrich 30, 31, 132–4
Heidegger, Martin 79, 89–91, 96, 98

history 20, 28, 34, 36, 55, 60–65, 67–9, 77, 79–80, 82, 84
human nature 44, 88
humanism 6, 11, 19, 27–30, 38

identity 1–5, 13, 18, 57–62, 67, 70–1, 75, 151
internet 3, 8, 41, 113–4, 145, 149, 150, 152–3
Irigaray, Luce 9–11, 13, 20–1

#JeSuisCharlie 1, 2, 4, 5, 6, 94

Lacan, Jacques 7, 102, 104–6, 110–2
lack 16, 55
limits 21, 36, 66

machine, the 4, 41, 103, 142, 143, 151
Marx, Karl 7, 31, 34–5, 142, 148
material 57, 81, 121, 151–2
memory 62, 147
Meschonnic, Henri 7–8, 117–9, 121–3, 125
#MeToo 3, 146, 156

Nancy, Jean-Luc 8, 86–93, 95–8, 134–5, 137–8
nature 9–10, 11–17, 19–21, 24, 27, 28, 31–4, 38, 44, 58, 64–6
Nietzsche, Friedrich 9–12, 21, 80, 105, 149
non-human, the 6, 27, 31–2, 37, 150
#NousSommes 1, 3–5, 7–8, 75, 80, 84, 129, 133–9, 155

other 1–4, 9–12, 15–7, 20–4, 27, 30–1, 33, 62, 64–5, 67, 71, 149

philosophy 5, 18, 81, 144
poetry 14, 98, 106, 117

queer 6, 12–4, 16–7, 19–24

rationality 29, 31, 67
reader 107, 117, 119, 126, 127
representation 14, 16, 32, 45–7, 51, 81, 83
Ricœur, Paul 49
Rousseau, Jean-Jacques 137

Sen, Amartya 147
social media 1–3, 7, 8, 18, 75, 76–9, 81–4, 142, 145, 151
Stiegler, Bernard 8, 81, 144–5, 147–9
subject 8, 9, 11, 13–4, 16–7, 20–1, 23, 36–7, 62, 146

subjectivity 6, 9, 15, 18–9, 23, 57, 76, 78–80, 82, 102, 119, 151

technology 7, 33, 55, 60, 62, 66–8, 75–6, 79, 82–3, 101, 142–3, 145–6, 148–9, 153–5
terrorism 2, 41, 48–52, 83, 86–7, 89, 92–4
torture 6, 14, 20, 22, 29, 36–8
Twitter 98

university 9, 24, 153

violence 1, 2, 49, 79, 82–3, 103, 115, 120, 123, 145–6
vulnerability 41, 50, 147

Modern French Identities
Edited by Jean Khalfa

This series aims to publish monographs, editions or collections of papers based on recent research into modern French Literature. It welcomes contributions from academics, researchers and writers worldwide and in British and Irish universities in particular.

Modern French Identities focuses on the French and Francophone writing of the twentieth and twenty-first centuries, whose formal experiments and revisions of genre have combined to create an entirely new set of literary forms, from the thematic autobiographies of Michel Leiris and Bernard Noël to the magic realism of French Caribbean writers.

The idea that identities are constructed rather than found, and that the self is an area to explore rather than a given pretext, runs through much of modern French literature, from Proust, Gide, Apollinaire and Césaire to Barthes, Duras, Kristeva, Glissant, Germain and Roubaud.

This series explores the turmoil in ideas and values expressed in the works of theorists like Lacan, Irigaray, Foucault, Fanon, Deleuze and Bourdieu and traces the impact of current theoretical approaches – such as gender and sexuality studies, de/coloniality, intersectionality, and ecocriticism – on the literary and cultural interpretation of the self.

The series publishes studies of individual authors and artists, comparative studies, and interdisciplinary projects and welcomes research on autobiography, cinema, fiction, poetry and performance art and/or the intersections between them.

Editorial Board

Contemporary Literature and Thought
Martin Crowley (University of Cambridge)

Francophone Studies
Louise Hardwick (University of Birmingham)
Jean Khalfa (University of Cambridge)

Gender and Sexuality Studies
Florian Grandena (University of Ottawa)
Cristina Johnston (University of Stirling)

Language and Linguistics
Michaël Abecassis (University of Oxford)

Literature and Art
Peter Collier and Jean Khalfa (University of Cambridge)

Literature and Non-fiction
Muriel Pic (University of Bern)

Poetry
Nina Parish (University of Bath)
Emma Wagstaff (University of Birmingham)

Zoopoetics and Ecocriticism
Anne Simon (CNRS/EHESS, Paris)

Volume 1   Victoria Best & Peter Collier (eds): Powerful Bodies.
          Performance in French Cultural Studies.
          220 pages. 1999. ISBN 3-906762-56-4 / US-ISBN 0-8204-4239-9

Volume 2   Julia Waters: Intersexual Rivalry.
          A 'Reading in Pairs' of Marguerite Duras and Alain Robbe-Grillet.
          228 pages. 2000. ISBN 3-906763-74-9 / US-ISBN 0-8204-4626-2

Volume 3   Sarah Cooper: Relating to Queer Theory.
          Rereading Sexual Self-Definition with Irigaray, Kristeva, Wittig
          and Cixous.
          231 pages. 2000. ISBN 3-906764-46-X / US-ISBN 0-8204-4636-X

Volume 4   Julia Prest & Hannah Thompson (eds): Corporeal Practices.
          (Re)figuring the Body in French Studies.
          166 pages. 2000. ISBN 3-906764-53-2 / US-ISBN 0-8204-4639-4

Volume 5   Victoria Best: Critical Subjectivities.
          Identity and Narrative in the Work
          of Colette and Marguerite Duras.
          243 pages. 2000. ISBN 3-906763-89-7 / US-ISBN 0-8204-4631-9

Volume 6   David Houston Jones: The Body Abject: Self and Text in
          Jean Genet and Samuel Beckett.
          213 pages. 2000. ISBN 3-906765-07-5 / US-ISBN 0-8204-5058-8

Volume 7   Robin MacKenzie: The Unconscious in Proust's *A la recherche
          du temps perdu*.
          270 pages. 2000. ISBN 3-906758-38-9 / US-ISBN 0-8204-5070-7

Volume 8   Rosemary Chapman: Siting the Quebec Novel.
          The Representation of Space in Francophone Writing in Quebec.
          282 pages. 2000. ISBN 3-906758-85-0 / US-ISBN 0-8204-5090-1

Volume 9   Gill Rye: Reading for Change.
          Interactions between Text Identity in Contemporary French
          Women's Writing (Baroche, Cixous, Constant).
          223 pages. 2001. ISBN 3-906765-97-0 / US-ISBN 0-8204-5315-3

Volume 10 Jonathan Paul Murphy: Proust's Art.
          Painting, Sculpture and Writing in *A la recherche du temps perdu*.
          248 pages. 2001. ISBN 3-906766-17-9 / US-ISBN 0-8204-5319-6

Volume 11 Julia Dobson: Hélène Cixous and the Theatre.
          The Scene of Writing.
          166 pages. 2002. ISBN 3-906766-20-9 / US-ISBN 0-8204-5322-6

Volume 12 Emily Butterworth & Kathryn Robson (eds): Shifting Borders.
          Theory and Identity in French Literature.
          226 pages. 2001.
          ISBN 3-906766-86-1 / US-ISBN 0-8204-5602-0

Volume 13   Victoria Korzeniowska: The Heroine as Social Redeemer in
            the Plays of Jean Giraudoux.
            144 pages. 2001. ISBN 3-906766-92-6 / US-ISBN 0-8204-5608-X

Volume 14   Kay Chadwick: Alphonse de Châteaubriant:
            Catholic Collaborator.
            327 pages. 2002. ISBN 3-906766-94-2 / US-ISBN 0-8204-5610-1

Volume 15   Nina Bastin: Queneau's Fictional Worlds.
            291 pages. 2002. ISBN 3-906768-32-5 / US-ISBN 0-8204-5620-9

Volume 16   Sarah Fishwick: The Body in the Work of Simone de Beauvoir.
            284 pages. 2002. ISBN 3-906768-33-3 / US-ISBN 0-8204-5621-7

Volume 17   Simon Kemp & Libby Saxton (eds): Seeing Things.
            Vision, Perception and Interpretation in French Studies.
            287 pages. 2002. ISBN 3-906768-46-5 / US-ISBN 0-8204-5858-9

Volume 18   Kamal Salhi (ed.): French in and out of France.
            Language Policies, Intercultural Antagonisms and Dialogue.
            487 pages. 2002. ISBN 3-906768-47-3 / US-ISBN 0-8204-5859-7

Volume 19   Genevieve Shepherd: Simone de Beauvoir's Fiction.
            A Psychoanalytic Rereading.
            262 pages. 2003. ISBN 3-906768-55-4 / US-ISBN 0-8204-5867-8

Volume 20   Lucille Cairns (ed.): Gay and Lesbian Cultures in France.
            290 pages. 2002. ISBN 3-906769-66-6 / US-ISBN 0-8204-5903-8

Volume 21   Wendy Goolcharan-Kumeta: My Mother, My Country.
            Reconstructing the Female Self in Guadeloupean Women's Writing.
            236 pages. 2003. ISBN 3-906769-76-3 / US-ISBN 0-8204-5913-5

Volume 22   Patricia O'Flaherty: Henry de Montherlant (1895–1972).
            A Philosophy of Failure.
            256 pages. 2003. ISBN 3-03910-013-0 / US-ISBN 0-8204-6282-9

Volume 23   Katherine Ashley (ed.): Prix Goncourt, 1903–2003: essais critiques.
            205 pages. 2004. ISBN 3-03910-018-1 / US-ISBN 0-8204-6287-X

Volume 24   Julia Horn & Lynsey Russell-Watts (eds): Possessions.
            Essays in French Literature, Cinema and Theory.
            223 pages. 2003. ISBN 3-03910-005-X / US-ISBN 0-8204-5924-0

Volume 25   Steve Wharton: Screening Reality.
            French Documentary Film during the German Occupation.
            252 pages. 2006. ISBN 3-03910-066-1 / US-ISBN 0-8204-6882-7

Volume 26   Frédéric Royall (ed.): Contemporary French Cultures and Societies.
            421 pages. 2004. ISBN 3-03910-074-2 / US-ISBN 0-8204-6890-8

Volume 27   Tom Genrich: Authentic Fictions.
            Cosmopolitan Writing of the Troisième République, 1908–1940.
            288 pages. 2004. ISBN 3-03910-285-0 / US-ISBN 0-8204-7212-3

Volume 28   Maeve Conrick & Vera Regan: French in Canada.
            Language Issues.
            186 pages. 2007. ISBN 978-3-03-910142-9

Volume 29   Kathryn Banks & Joseph Harris (eds): Exposure.
            Revealing Bodies, Unveiling Representations.
            194 pages. 2004. ISBN 3-03910-163-3 / US-ISBN 0-8204-6973-4

Volume 30   Emma Gilby & Katja Haustein (eds): Space.
            New Dimensions in French Studies.
            169 pages. 2005. ISBN 3-03910-178-1 / US-ISBN 0-8204-6988-2

Volume 31   Rachel Killick (ed.): Uncertain Relations.
            Some Configurations of the 'Third Space' in Francophone Writings
            of the Americas and of Europe.
            258 pages. 2005. ISBN 3-03910-189-7 / US-ISBN 0-8204-6999-8

Volume 32   Sarah F. Donachie & Kim Harrison (eds): Love and Sexuality.
            New Approaches in French Studies.
            194 pages. 2005. ISBN 3-03910-249-4 / US-ISBN 0-8204-7178-X

Volume 33   Michaël Abecassis: The Representation of Parisian Speech in
            the Cinema of the 1930s.
            409 pages. 2005. ISBN 3-03910-260-5 / US-ISBN 0-8204-7189-5

Volume 34   Benedict O'Donohoe: Sartre's Theatre: Acts for Life.
            301 pages. 2005. ISBN 3-03910-250-X / US-ISBN 0-8204-7207-7

Volume 35   Moya Longstaffe: The Fiction of Albert Camus. A Complex Simplicity.
            300 pages. 2007. ISBN 3-03910-304-0 / US-ISBN 0-8204-7229-8

Volume 36   Arnaud Beaujeu: Matière et lumière dans le théâtre de Samuel Beckett:
            Autour des notions de trivialité, de spiritualité et d'« autre-là ».
            377 pages. 2010. ISBN 978-3-0343-0206-8

Volume 37   Shirley Ann Jordan: Contemporary French Women's Writing:
            Women's Visions, Women's Voices, Women's Lives.
            308 pages. 2005. ISBN 3-03910-315-6 / US-ISBN 0-8204-7240-9

Volume 38   Neil Foxlee: Albert Camus's 'The New Mediterranean Culture':
            A Text and its Contexts.
            349 pages. 2010. ISBN 978-3-0343-0207-4

Volume 39   Michael O'Dwyer & Michèle Raclot: Le Journal de Julien Green:
            Miroir d'une âme, miroir d'un siècle.
            289 pages. 2005. ISBN 3-03910-319-9

Volume 40	Thomas Baldwin: The Material Object in the Work of Marcel Proust. 188 pages. 2005. ISBN 3-03910-323-7 / US-ISBN 0-8204-7247-6
Volume 41	Charles Forsdick & Andrew Stafford (eds): The Modern Essay in French: Genre, Sociology, Performance. 296 pages. 2005. ISBN 3-03910-514-0 / US-ISBN 0-8204-7520-3
Volume 42	Peter Dunwoodie: Francophone Writing in Transition. Algeria 1900–1945. 339 pages. 2005. ISBN 3-03910-294-X / US-ISBN 0-8204-7220-4
Volume 43	Emma Webb (ed.): Marie Cardinal: New Perspectives. 260 pages. 2006. ISBN 3-03910-544-2 / US-ISBN 0-8204-7547-5
Volume 44	Jérôme Game (ed.): Porous Boundaries: Texts and Images in Twentieth-Century French Culture. 164 pages. 2007. ISBN 978-3-03910-568-7
Volume 45	David Gascoigne: The Games of Fiction: Georges Perec and Modern French Ludic Narrative. 327 pages. 2006. ISBN 3-03910-697-X / US-ISBN 0-8204-7962-4
Volume 46	Derek O'Regan: Postcolonial Echoes and Evocations: The Intertextual Appeal of Maryse Condé. 329 pages. 2006. ISBN 3-03910-578-7
Volume 47	Jennifer Hatte: La langue secrète de Jean Cocteau: la *mythologie personnelle* du poète et l'histoire cachée des *Enfants terribles*. 332 pages. 2007. ISBN 978-3-03910-707-0
Volume 48	Loraine Day: Writing Shame and Desire: The Work of Annie Ernaux. 315 pages. 2007. ISBN 978-3-03910-275-4
Volume 49	John Flower (éd.): François Mauriac, journaliste: les vingt premières années, 1905–1925. 352 pages. 2011. ISBN 978-3-0343-0265-4
Volume 50	Miriam Heywood: Modernist Visions: Marcel Proust's *A la recherche du temps perdu* and Jean-Luc Godard's *Histoire(s) du cinéma*. 277 pages. 2012. ISBN 978-3-0343-0296-8
Volume 51	Isabelle McNeill & Bradley Stephens (eds): Transmissions: Essays in French Literature, Thought and Cinema. 221 pages. 2007. ISBN 978-3-03910-734-6
Volume 52	Marie-Christine Lala: Georges Bataille, Poète du réel. 178 pages. 2010. ISBN 978-3-03910-738-4
Volume 53	Patrick Crowley: Pierre Michon: The Afterlife of Names. 242 pages. 2007. ISBN 978-3-03910-744-5

Volume 54   Nicole Thatcher & Ethel Tolansky (eds): Six Authors in Captivity. Literary Responses to the Occupation of France during World War II.
205 pages. 2006. ISBN 3-03910-520-5 / US-ISBN 0-8204-7526-2

Volume 55   Catherine Dousteyssier-Khoze & Floriane Place-Verghnes (eds): Poétiques de la parodie et du pastiche de 1850 à nos jours.
361 pages. 2006. ISBN 3-03910-743-7

Volume 56   Thanh-Vân Ton-That: Proust avant la *Recherche*: jeunesse et genèse d'une écriture au tournant du siècle.
285 pages. 2012. ISBN 978-3-0343-0277-7

Volume 57   Helen Vassallo: Jeanne Hyvrard, Wounded Witness: The Body Politic and the Illness Narrative.
243 pages. 2007. ISBN 978-3-03911-017-9

Volume 58   Marie-Claire Barnet, Eric Robertson and Nigel Saint (eds): Robert Desnos. Surrealism in the Twenty-First Century.
390 pages. 2006. ISBN 3-03911-019-5

Volume 59   Michael O'Dwyer (ed.): Julien Green, Diariste et Essayiste.
259 pages. 2007. ISBN 978-3-03911-016-2

Volume 60   Kate Marsh: Fictions of 1947: Representations of Indian Decolonization 1919–1962.
238 pages. 2007. ISBN 978-3-03911-033-9

Volume 61   Lucy Bolton, Gerri Kimber, Ann Lewis and Michael Seabrook (eds): Framed!: Essays in French Studies.
235 pages. 2007. ISBN 978-3-03911-043-8

Volume 62   Lorna Milne and Mary Orr (eds): Narratives of French Modernity: Themes, Forms and Metamorphoses. Essays in Honour of David Gascoigne.
365 pages. 2011. ISBN 978-3-03911-051-3

Volume 63   Ann Kennedy Smith: Painted Poetry: Colour in Baudelaire's Art Criticism.
253 pages. 2011. ISBN 978-3-03911-094-0

Volume 64   Sam Coombes: The Early Sartre and Marxism.
330 pages. 2008. ISBN 978-3-03911-115-2

Volume 65   Claire Lozier: De l'abject et du sublime: Georges Bataille, Jean Genet, Samuel Beckett.
327 pages. 2012. ISBN 978-3-0343-0724-6

Volume 66   Charles Forsdick and Andy Stafford (eds): *La Revue*: The Twentieth-Century Periodical in French.
379 pages. 2013. ISBN 978-3-03910-947-0

Volume 67	Alison S. Fell (ed.): French and francophone women facing war / Les femmes face à la guerre. 301 pages. 2009. ISBN 978-3-03911-332-3
Volume 68	Elizabeth Lindley and Laura McMahon (eds): Rhythms: Essays in French Literature, Thought and Culture. 238 pages. 2008. ISBN 978-3-03911-349-1
Volume 69	Georgina Evans and Adam Kay (eds): Threat: Essays in French Literature, Thought and Visual Culture. 248 pages. 2010. ISBN 978-3-03911-357-6
Volume 70	John McCann: Michel Houellebecq: Author of our Times. 229 pages. 2010. ISBN 978-3-03911-373-6
Volume 71	Jenny Murray: Remembering the (Post)Colonial Self: Memory and Identity in the Novels of Assia Djebar. 258 pages. 2008. ISBN 978-3-03911-367-5
Volume 72	Susan Bainbrigge: Culture and Identity in Belgian Francophone Writing: Dialogue, Diversity and Displacement. 230 pages. 2009. ISBN 978-3-03911-382-8
Volume 73	Maggie Allison and Angela Kershaw (eds): *Parcours de femmes*: Twenty Years of Women in French. 313 pages. 2011. ISBN 978-3-0343-0208-1
Volume 74	Jérôme Game: Poetic Becomings: Studies in Contemporary French Literature. 263 pages. 2011. ISBN 978-3-03911-401-6
Volume 75	Elodie Laügt: L'Orient du signe: Rêves et dérives chez Victor Segalen, Henri Michaux et Emile Cioran. 242 pages. 2008. ISBN 978-3-03911-402-3
Volume 76	Suzanne Dow: Madness in Twentieth-Century French Women's Writing: Leduc, Duras, Beauvoir, Cardinal, Hyvrard. 217 pages. 2009. ISBN 978-3-03911-540-2
Volume 77	Myriem El Maïzi: Marguerite Duras ou l'écriture du devenir. 228 pages. 2009. ISBN 978-3-03911-561-7
Volume 78	Claire Launchbury: Music, Poetry, Propaganda: Constructing French Cultural Soundscapes at the BBC during the Second World War. 223 pages. 2012. ISBN 978-3-0343-0239-5
Volume 79	Jenny Chamarette and Jennifer Higgins (eds): Guilt and Shame: Essays in French Literature, Thought and Visual Culture. 231 pages. 2010. ISBN 978-3-03911-563-1

Volume 80	Vera Regan and Caitríona Ní Chasaide (eds): Language Practices and Identity Construction by Multilingual Speakers of French L2: The Acquisition of Sociostylistic Variation. 189 pages. 2010. ISBN 978-3-03911-569-3
Volume 81	Margaret-Anne Hutton (ed.): Redefining the Real: The Fantastic in Contemporary French and Francophone Women's Writing. 294 pages. 2009. ISBN 978-3-03911-567-9
Volume 82	Elise Hugueny-Léger: Annie Ernaux, une poétique de la transgression. 269 pages. 2009. ISBN 978-3-03911-833-5
Volume 83	Peter Collier, Anna Magdalena Elsner and Olga Smith (eds): Anamnesia: Private and Public Memory in Modern French Culture. 359 pages. 2009. ISBN 978-3-03911-846-5
Volume 84	Adam Watt (ed./éd.): Le Temps retrouvé Eighty Years After/80 ans après: Critical Essays/Essais critiques. 349 pages. 2009. ISBN 978-3-03911-843-4
Volume 85	Louise Hardwick (ed.): New Approaches to Crime in French Literature, Culture and Film. 237 pages. 2009. ISBN 978-3-03911-850-2
Volume 86	Emmanuel Godin and Natalya Vince (eds): France and the Mediterranean: International Relations, Culture and Politics. 372 pages. 2012. ISBN 978-3-0343-0228-9
Volume 87	Amaleena Damlé and Aurélie L'Hostis (eds): The Beautiful and the Monstrous: Essays in French Literature, Thought and Culture. 237 pages. 2010. ISBN 978-3-03911-900-4
Volume 88	Alistair Rolls (ed.): Mostly French: French (in) Detective Fiction. 212 pages. 2009. ISBN 978-3-03911-957-8
Volume 89	Bérénice Bonhomme: Claude Simon: une écriture en cinéma. 359 pages. 2010. ISBN 978-3-03911-983-7
Volume 90	Barbara Lebrun and Jill Lovecy (eds): *Une et divisible?* Plural Identities in Modern France. 258 pages. 2010. ISBN 978-3-0343-0123-7
Volume 91	Pierre-Alexis Mével & Helen Tattam (eds): Language and its Contexts/ Le Langage et ses contextes: Transposition and Transformation of Meaning?/Transposition et transformation du sens ? 272 pages. 2010. ISBN 978-3-0343-0128-2
Volume 92	Alistair Rolls and Marie-Laure Vuaille-Barcan (eds): Masking Strategies: Unwrapping the French Paratext. 202 pages. 2011. ISBN 978-3-0343-0746-8

Volume 93   Michaël Abecassis et Gudrun Ledegen (éds): Les Voix des Français
             Volume 1: à travers l'histoire, l'école et la presse.
             372 pages. 2010. ISBN 978-3-0343-0170-1

Volume 94   Michaël Abecassis et Gudrun Ledegen (éds): Les Voix des Français
             Volume 2: en parlant, en écrivant.
             481 pages. 2010. ISBN 978-3-0343-0171-8

Volume 95   Manon Mathias, Maria O'Sullivan and Ruth Vorstman (eds): Display
             and Disguise.
             237 pages. 2011. ISBN 978-3-0343-0177-0

Volume 96   Charlotte Baker: Enduring Negativity: Representations of Albinism in
             the Novels of Didier Destremau, Patrick Grainville and Williams Sassine.
             226 pages. 2011. ISBN 978-3-0343-0179-4

Volume 97   Florian Grandena and Cristina Johnston (eds): New Queer Images:
             Representations of Homosexualities in Contemporary Francophone
             Visual Cultures.
             246 pages. 2011. ISBN 978-3-0343-0182-4

Volume 98   Florian Grandena and Cristina Johnston (eds): Cinematic Queerness:
             Gay and Lesbian Hypervisibility in Contemporary Francophone
             Feature Films.
             354 pages. 2011. ISBN 978-3-0343-0183-1

Volume 99   Neil Archer and Andreea Weisl-Shaw (eds): Adaptation: Studies in
             French and Francophone Culture.
             234 pages. 2012. ISBN 978-3-0343-0222-7

Volume 100   Peter Collier et Ilda Tomas (éds): Béatrice Bonhomme: le mot, la
             mort, l'amour.
             437 pages. 2013. ISBN 978-3-0343-0780-2

Volume 101   Helena Chadderton: Marie Darrieussecq's Textual Worlds: Self,
             Society, Language.
             170 pages. 2012. ISBN 978-3-0343-0766-6

Volume 102   Manuel Bragança: La crise allemande du roman français, 1945–1949:
             la représentation des Allemands dans les *best-sellers* de l'immédiat
             après-guerre.
             220 pages. 2012. ISBN 978-3-0343-0835-9

Volume 103   Bronwen Martin: The Fiction of J. M. G. Le Clézio: A Postcolonial
             Reading.
             199 pages. 2012. ISBN 978-3-0343-0162-6

Volume 104   Hugues Azérad, Michael G. Kelly, Nina Parish et Emma Wagstaff (éds):
             Chantiers du poème: prémisses et pratiques de la création poétique
             moderne et contemporaine.
             374 pages. 2013. ISBN 978-3-0343-0800-7

Volume 105 Franck Dalmas: Lectures phénoménologiques en littérature française: de Gustave Flaubert à Malika Mokeddem.
253 pages. 2012. ISBN 978-3-0343-0727-7

Volume 106 Béatrice Bonhomme, Aude Préta-de Beaufort et Jacques Moulin (éds): Dans le feuilletage de la terre: sur l'œuvre poétique de Marie-Claire Bancquart.
533 pages. 2013. ISBN 978-3-0343-0721-5

Volume 107 Claire Bisdorff et Marie-Christine Clemente (éds): Le Cœur dans tous ses états: essais sur la littérature et l'art français.
230 pages. 2013. ISBN 978-3-0343-0711-6

Volume 108 Michaël Abecassis et Gudrun Ledegen (éds): Écarts et apports des médias francophones: lexique et grammaire.
300 pages. 2013. ISBN 978-3-0343-0882-3

Volume 109 Maggie Allison and Imogen Long (eds): Women Matter / *Femmes Matière*: French and Francophone Women and the Material World.
273 pages. 2013. ISBN 978-3-0343-0788-8

Volume 110 Fabien Arribert-Narce et Alain Ausoni (éds): L'Autobiographie entre autres: écrire la vie aujourd'hui.
221 pages. 2013. ISBN 978-3-0343-0858-8

Volume 111 Leona Archer and Alex Stuart (eds): Visions of Apocalypse: Representations of the End in French Literature and Culture.
266 pages. 2013. ISBN 978-3-0343-0921-9

Volume 112 Simona Cutcan: Subversion ou conformisme? La différence des sexes dans l'œuvre d'Agota Kristof.
264 pages. 2014. ISBN 978-3-0343-1713-9

Volume 113 Owen Heathcote: From Bad Boys to New Men? Masculinity, Sexuality and Violence in the Work of Éric Jourdan.
279 pages. 2014. ISBN 978-3-0343-0736-9

Volume 114 Ilda Tomas: Arc-en-ciel: études sur divers poètes.
234 pages. 2014. ISBN 978-3-0343-0975-2

Volume 115 Lisa Jeschke and Adrian May (eds): Matters of Time: Material Temporalities in Twentieth-Century French Culture.
314 pages. 2014. ISBN 978-3-0343-1796-2

Volume 116 Crispin T. Lee: Haptic Experience in the Writings of Georges Bataille, Maurice Blanchot and Michel Serres.
316 pages. 2014. ISBN 978-3-0343-1791-7

Volume 117 Ashwiny O. Kistnareddy: Locating Hybridity: Creole, Identities and Body Politics in the Novels of Ananda Devi.
208 pages. 2015. ISBN 978-3-0343-1814-3

Volume 118 Michaël Abecassis et Gudrun Ledegen (éds): De la genèse de la langue à Internet: variations dans les formes, les modalités et les langues en contact.
278 pages. 2015. ISBN 978-3-0343-1798-6

Volume 119 Peter D. Tame: Isotopias: Places and Spaces in French War Fiction of the Twentieth and Twenty-First Centuries.
592 pages. 2015. ISBN 978-3-0343-0837-3

Volume 120 Daniel A. Finch-Race et Jeff Barda (éds): Textures: Processus et événements dans la création poétique moderne et contemporaine.
242 pages. 2015. ISBN 978-3-0343-1898-3

Volume 121 Hélène Sicard-Cowan: Vivre ensemble: éthique de l'imitation dans la littérature et le cinéma de l'immigration en France (1986–2005).
149 pages. 2016. ISBN 978-3-0343-1944-7

Volume 122 Mercedes Montoro Araque et Carmen Alberdi Urquizu (éds): L'entre-deux imaginaire: corps et création interculturels.
216 pages. 2016. ISBN 978-3-0343-1926-3

Volume 123 Maureen A. Ramsden: Crossing Borders: The Interrelation of Fact and Fiction in Historical Works, Travel Tales, Autobiography and Reportage.
191 pages. 2016. ISBN 978-3-0343-1995-9

Volume 124 Jean Khalfa: Poetics of the Antilles: Poetry, History and Philosophy in the Writings of Perse, Césaire, Fanon and Glissant.
388 pages. 2017. ISBN 978-3-0343-0895-3

Volume 125 Mathilde Poizat-Amar: L'Eclat du voyage: Blaise Cendrars, Victor Segalen, Albert Londres.
252 pages. 2017. ISBN 978-1-78707-296-1

Volume 126 Philippe Willemart: L'Univers de la création littéraire: Dans la chambre noire de l'écriture : *Hérodias* de Flaubert.
160 pages. 2017. ISBN 978-1-78707-458-3

Volume 127 Margaret Atack, Alison S. Fell, Diana Holmes and Imogen Long (eds): French Feminisms 1975 and After: New Readings, New Texts.
276 pages. 2018. ISBN 978-3-0343-2209-6

Volume 128 Matt Phillips and Tomas Weber (eds): Parasites: Exploitation and Interference in French Thought and Culture.
284 pages. 2018. ISBN 978-3-0343-2266-9

Volume 129 Zoe Angelis and Blake Gutt (eds): Stains / Les taches: Communication and Contamination in French and Francophone Literature and Culture.
274 pages. 2019. ISBN 978-1-78707-443-9

Volume 130 Michaël Abecassis avec Marcelline Block, Gudrun Ledegen et Maribel Peñalver Vicea (éds): Le Grain de la voix dans le monde anglophone et francophone.
332 pages. 2019. ISBN 978-1-78874-107-1

Volume 131 Philippe Willemart: L'écriture à l'ère de l'indétermination : Études sur la critique génétique, la psychanalyse et la littérature.
232 pages. 2019. ISBN 978–1-78874-631-1

Volume 132 Augustin Voegele : De l'unanimisme au fantastique : Jules Romains devant l'extraordinaire.
382 pages. 2019. ISBN 978-1-78874-513-0

Volume 133 Maggie Allison, Elliot Evans and Carrie Tarr (eds): *Plaisirs de femmes*: Women, Pleasure and Transgression in French Literature and Culture.
278 pages. 2019. ISBN 978-1-78874-383-9

Volume 134 Aaron Prevots: Bernard Vargaftig: Gestures toward the Sacred.
144 pages. 2019. ISBN 978-1-78997-357-0

Volume 135 Susie Cronin, Sofia Ropek Hewson and Cillian Ó Fathaigh (eds): #NousSommes: Collectivity and the Digital in French Thought and Culture. xxxx pages. 2020. ISBN 978-1-78874-767-7

www.ingramcontent.com/pod-product-compliance
Ingram Content Group UK Ltd.
Pitfield, Milton Keynes, MK11 3LW, UK
UKHW021846140426
5217IPUK00022B/1618